63 Tactics for Teaching Diverse Learners K–6

To all teachers and those they teach . . .

63 Tactics for Teaching Diverse Learners K–6

Bob Algozzine
Pam Campbell
Adam Wang

CORWIN PRESS
A SAGE Company

For information:

Corwin Press
A SAGE Company
2455 Teller Road
Thousand Oaks, California 91320
www.corwinpress.com

SAGE Ltd.
1 Oliver's Yard
55 City Road
London EC1Y 1SP
United Kingdom

SAGE India Pvt. Ltd.
B 1/I 1 Mohan Cooperative
   Industrial Area
Mathura Road, New Delhi 110 044
India

SAGE Asia-Pacific Pte. Ltd.
33 Pekin Street #02-01
Far East Square
Singapore 048763

Printed in the United States of America.

Library of Congress Cataloging-in-Publication Data

Algozzine, Robert.
63 tactics for teaching diverse learners, K–6 / Bob Algozzine, Pamela Campbell, Adam Wang.
     p. cm.
Includes bibliographical references.
ISBN 978-1-4129-4237-9 (cloth)
ISBN 978-1-4129-4238-6 (pbk.)
   1. Elementary school teaching. 2. Effective teaching. I. Campbell, Pam, 1942-
II. Wang, Adam, 1956- III. Title. IV. Title: Sixty-three tactics for teaching diverse learners, K–6.

LB1555.A545 2009
372.1102—dc22   2008035120

This book is printed on acid-free paper.

08   09   10   11   12   10 9 8 7 6 5 4 3 2 1

Acquisitions Editor:	David Chao
Editorial Assistant:	Mary Dang and Brynn Saito
Production Editor:	Eric Garner
Copy Editor:	Paula L. Fleming
Typesetter:	C&M Digitals (P) Ltd.
Proofreader:	Susan Schon
Indexer:	Ellen Slavitz
Cover Designer:	Rose Storey
Graphic Designer:	Monique Hahn

Contents

Preface

As students with disabilities and learning differences are included in general education settings in greater numbers and for longer periods of time, educators—expert and novice alike—are searching for ways to meet individual needs most effectively. While many recognize that a teacher's expertise is often the critical determinant in any student's achievement, they also realize that meeting the increasingly diverse needs of students calls for additional information and support. In this regard, teachers need easy and simple access to authentic information about teaching and responding to individual differences effectively.

Effective Teaching

63 Tactics for Teaching Diverse Learners, K–6 is a collection of evidence-based practices designed to help teachers address the instructional needs present in America's classrooms. The book is organized around four components of effective instruction: planning, managing, delivering, and evaluating (cf. Algozzine & Ysseldyke, 1992; Algozzine, Ysseldyke, & Elliott, 1997). It is based on a fundamental belief: teachers are able to respond to individual differences more effectively when provided with an easily accessible resource of effective tactics.

63 Tactics for Teaching Diverse Learners, K–6 provides all teachers (regardless of level, experience, or area of specialization) with access to effective instructional tactics. In developing this book, we used a peer review process that encouraged flexibility and resulted in a collection of teaching activities that help teachers to meet the needs of students in diverse classroom and school settings. *63 Tactics for Teaching Diverse Learners, K–6* is based on sound models of instruction, and its structure encourages the identification and use of practices that are effective for students with or without disabilities, as well as practices that are designed especially for students with disabilities at all grade levels.

Ecological Validity

Ecological validity refers to the extent to which the underlying constructs of an educational model are grounded in logical, representative, and important conditions within the real world of schools. It is a measure of the value, worth, or projected effectiveness of the model. The ecological validity, or usefulness, of the activities is grounded in considering five assumptions:

1. All children want to learn.

    Ask any child.

2. All children can learn.

    Ask any parent.

3. All schools can educate diverse groups of students.

    Ask any administrator.

4. All classrooms are places where students with varying instructional needs can learn.
   Ask any teacher.

5. All teachers want to teach well so students will learn and succeed; all they need is time, access to information, and sustained support.
   Ask anybody.

Underlying Model

63 Tactics for Teaching Diverse Learners, K–6 is based on a practical model in which four components (i.e., planning, managing, delivering, and evaluating) serve as the basis for a set of organizing principles of effective instruction (see below).

Components and Principles of Effective Instruction

Component	Principle
Planning	Decide What to Teach Decide How to Teach Communicate Realistic Expectations
Managing	Prepare for Instruction Use Time Productively Establish Positive Classroom Environment
Delivering	Present Information Monitor Presentations Adjust Presentations
Evaluating	Monitor Student Understanding Monitor Engaged Time Keep Records of Student Progress Use Data to Make Decisions

SOURCE: Algozzine et al., 1997

To bring the model to life and address the ever-present concern of administrators and teachers for implementation assistance, each component and principle is embodied by a set of strategies, which represent plans for action in putting theory into practice (see below).

Component	Principle	Strategy
Planning	Decide What to Teach	Assess to Identify Gaps in Performance Establish Logical Sequences of Instruction Consider Contextual Variables
	Decide How to Teach	Set Instructional Goals Establish Performance Standards Choose Instructional Methods and Materials Establish Grouping Structures Pace Instruction Appropriately Monitor Performance and Replan Instruction
	Communicate Realistic Expectations	Teach Goals, Objectives, and Standards Teach Students to Be Active, Involved Learners Teach Students Consequences of Performance

SOURCE: Algozzine et al., 1997

Strategies are steps that should be taken to implement principles and components of effective instruction; they are the *what* rather than the *how* of teaching. Tactics are actions that a teacher can take to influence learning (i.e., the *how* of effective teaching). They are the lowest level a component can be broken into for instructional purposes; they are specific behaviors or teaching activities (see below).

Organizational Relations in Algozzine and Ysseldyke Model	
Component:	Delivering Instruction
Principle:	Monitor Presentations
Strategy:	Provide Prompts and Cues
Tactic:	*Use Signals to Request Help:* Develop a signal for each student to use when assistance is needed during an independent practice session. Circulate through the room when students are practicing and look for signs that someone needs help. Provide help as quickly as possible so that students can continue to work.

SOURCE: Algozzine et al., 1997

Algozzine and Ysseldyke (1992) and Algozzine et al. (1997) used the model as a base for a collection of evidence-based tactics to help teachers teach more effectively. In *63 Tactics for Teaching Diverse Learners, K–6*, we have compiled additional tactics drawn from a review of professional publications and from extensive observations of experienced teachers and other professionals who teach students with disabilities and diverse learning needs in general education classrooms. We grouped them according to the components and principles of effective instruction identified by Algozzine and Ysseldyke (see below).

Components, Principles, and Strategies for Effective Instruction

Component	Principle	Strategy
Planning Instruction	Decide What to Teach	Assess to Identify Gaps in Performance Establish Logical Sequences of Instruction Consider Contextual Variables
	Decide How to Teach	Set Instructional Goals Establish Performance Standards Choose Instructional Methods and Materials Establish Grouping Structures Pace Instruction Appropriately Monitor Performance and Replan Instruction
	Communicate Realistic Expectations	Teach Goals, Objectives, and Standards Teach Students to Be Active, Involved Learners Teach Students Consequences of Performance
Managing Instruction	Prepare for Instruction	Set Classroom Rules Communicate and Teach Classroom Rules Communicate Consequences of Behavior Handle Disruptions Efficiently Teach Students to Manage Their Own Behavior
	Use Time Productively	Establish Routines and Procedures Organize Physical Space Allocate Sufficient Time to Academic Activities
	Establish Positive Classroom Environment	Make the Classroom a Pleasant, Friendly Place Accept Individual Differences Establish Supportive Learning Environments Create a Nonthreatening Learning Environment

(Continued)

(Continued)

Delivering Instruction	Present Information	Gain and Maintain Attention Review Prior Skills or Lessons Provide Organized, Relevant Lessons
		Show Enthusiasm and Interest Use Rewards Effectively Consider Level and Student Interest
		Model Thinking Skills Teach Fact-Finding Skills Teach Divergent Thinking Teach Learning Strategies
		Develop Automaticity Vary Opportunities for Practice Vary Methods of Practice Monitor Amount of Work Assigned
	Monitor Presentations	Give Immediate, Frequent, Explicit Feedback Provide Specific Praise and Encouragement Model Correct Performance Provide Prompts and Cues Check Student Understanding
		Monitor Performance Regularly Monitor Performance During Practice Use Peers to Improve Instruction Provide Opportunities for Success Limit Opportunities for Failure Monitor Engagement Rates
	Adjust Presentations	Adapt Lessons to Meet Student Needs Provide Varied Instructional Options Alter Pace
Evaluating Instruction	Monitor Student Understanding	Check Understanding of Directions Check Procedural Understanding Monitor Student Success Rate
	Monitor Engaged Time	Check Student Participation Teach Students to Monitor Their Own Participation
	Keep Records of Student Progress	Teach Students to Chart Their Own Progress Regularly Inform Students of Performance Maintain Records of Student Performance
	Use Data to Make Decisions	Use Data to Decide If More Services Are Warranted Use Student Progress to Make Teaching Decisions Use Student Progress to Decide When to Discontinue Service

SOURCE: Algozzine & Ysseldyke, 1992; Algozzine et al., 1997

63 Tactics for Teaching Diverse Learners, K–6 is based on a fundamental belief: teachers are able to respond to individual differences more effectively when provided with an easily accessible resource of effective tactics. *63 Tactics for Teaching Diverse Learners, K–6* responds to two fundamental problems in education: regardless of certification area, (1) very few teachers receive sufficient experience during student teaching or practicum experiences in identifying or using evidence-based tactics of effective instruction, and (2) very few teachers receive instruction in or have access to specific tactics for addressing instructional diversity and meeting individual needs in their classrooms. *63 Tactics for Teaching Diverse Learners, K–6* also responds to a widespread need in today's classrooms.

Most teachers agree: they often do not have enough time to meet all the needs of all their students effectively. Thus, time is an ongoing and primary need. *63 Tactics for Teaching Diverse Learners, K–6* addresses this need by providing teachers with quick access to reliable information about effective instructional tactics, regardless of their area of expertise or the diverse needs of their students. When using the book, teachers have several options:

- Identifying a problem and searching for solutions using the model of effective instruction, grade level, content area, category of student disability, and/or type of student learning difference.
- Searching without referencing a problem or any aspects of it.
- Examining the knowledge base underlying each tactic.
- Noting items from the database for later use.
- Implementing tactics.
- Evaluating and revising instructional plans using the model and specific tactics.

Where to Go From Here

Teachers are daily faced with questions that must be addressed if they are to be effective with all children.

I teach students in an elementary school. My specialty is history and mathematics. How can I develop appropriate learning activities for a student with learning disabilities? How can I arrange my instruction to accommodate students with a deficit in short-term memory? How can I improve my ongoing assessment of student learning? How do I use data to make decisions?

63 Tactics for Teaching Diverse Learners, K–6 helps teachers to associate a problem with an easily accessible set of solutions. It helps teachers move from questions to answers in a rapid and organized manner. It is unique in that we not only provide classroom-tested tactics for effective instruction for students with disabilities, but we also substantiate them with relevant and related literature. Thus, teachers can be assured of implementing evidence-based practices grounded in ongoing research. Many tactics and worksheets are applicable across the model, content areas, learning differences and disability categories. We also provide feedback, comments, and examples from practicing teachers, who offer practical suggestions as to how tactics might be modified and/or enhanced in terms of their content or application.

Acknowledgments

No one writes a book without help and support from others, and we are no exception. When we began this project, our goal was to share what we had learned from working with teachers and their students around the country. We are thankful for that experience and for what they and our own students continually taught us. We are also grateful to our colleagues who, by way of conducting and reporting their research, have provided an ever-renewing resource of evidence-based practices for helping diverse learners to succeed in school. We also acknowledge the very professional support of David Chao, Mary Dang, and Kathleen McLane at Corwin Press who kept us on track and contributed greatly to every part of producing this book.

Corwin Press would also like to thank the following for contributions to this book:

Roxie Ahlbrecht
2nd Grade Classroom Teacher/Math Teacher-Leader
Robert Frost Elementary/Sioux Falls Public Schools
Sioux Falls, SD

Nicole Guyon
Special Education Teacher
Westerly School Department
Cranston, RI

About the Authors

Bob Algozzine, PhD, from Penn State University, is codirector of the Behavior and Reading Improvement Center and professor of educational administration, research, and technology at the University of North Carolina at Charlotte. He is the coauthor of *Strategies and Tactics for Effective Instruction, Critical Issues in Special and Remedial Education, Introduction to Special Education,* and other college textbooks. He has published more than 250 articles on effective teaching, assessment, special education issues, and improving the lives of individuals with disabilities. His recent research has been published in the *High School Journal,* the *Journal of Educational Research,* and *Teacher Education and Special Education.* He has been a special education classroom teacher and college professor for more than 30 years in public schools and universities in New York, Virginia, Pennsylvania, Florida, and North Carolina. For nine years, he was coeditor, with Martha Thurlow, of *Exceptional Children,* the premiere research journal in the field of special education. He is currently the coeditor of *Teacher Education and Special Education, The Journal of Special Education,* and *Career Development for Exceptional Individuals.*

Pam Campbell, PhD, from University of Florida, is an associate professor in the Department of Special Education at the University of Nevada—Las Vegas (UNLV). During her 35 years as an educator, she has taught university courses in instruction, assessment, curriculum, and classroom management for both general and special educators. In addition, she has been a public school teacher in general education, Chapter I, and special education classrooms. She served in the dual role of university professor and coordinator of seven Professional Development Schools (PDS) at the University of Connecticut and currently at UNLV as coordinator of the Paradise PDS. Her research interests focus on linking the preparation of teacher candidates and sustained professional development of practicing teachers through technology. Her work has been published in *TEACHING Exceptional Children, Remedial and Special Education, Record in Educational Leadership, the Professional Educator,* and the *Council for Administrators of Special Education.* She is also the coauthor of *Improving Social Competence: Techniques for Elementary Teachers.* She has served the field of special education through numerous local, state, regional, and national presentations and as field reviewer for *Exceptional Children,* the *Journal of Special Education Technology, TEACHING Exceptional Children,* and *Teacher Education and Special Education.*

Jianjun (Adam) Wang, MA from University of Connecticut, is senior instructional technology specialist at Williams College. He has been responsible for collaborating with Campbell, Algozzine, and Ysseldyke in the design and development of STRIDE, the database that provided the foundation for this book. He has also been instrumental in the implementation of STRIDE in the preparation of future teachers, as well as the ongoing professional development of practicing educators. He has served as an instructor in technology courses and made several regional, national, and international conference presentations related to the effective implementation of technology in education. His research interests concern how educational technology can enhance human learning and focus on developing Web-based learning and teaching tools to enhance the undergraduate learning experience.

PART I

Planning Instruction

Effective teachers carefully plan their instruction. They decide *what to teach* and *how to teach* it. They also *communicate their expectations* for learning to their students. In this part of our resource, we describe evidenced-based strategies for each principle of planning instruction.

Component	Principle	Strategy
Planning Instruction (Part I)	Decide What to Teach (Chapter 1)	Assess to Identify Gaps in Performance
		Establish Logical Sequences of Instruction
		Consider Contextual Variables
	Decide How to Teach (Chapter 2)	Set Instructional Goals
		Establish Performance Standards
		Choose Instructional Methods and Materials
		Establish Grouping Structures
		Pace Instruction Appropriately
		Monitor Performance and Replan Instruction
	Communicate Realistic Expectations (Chapter 3)	Teach Goals, Objectives, and Standards
		Teach Students to Be Active, Involved Learners
		Teach Students Consequences of Performance

Planning Instruction Works: A Case Study

I've always considered myself an excellent planner, regardless of the fact that my principal reviews my plan book every Friday. I really want to be organized and prepared; you know, you have to be with 27 fifth graders in one room. So I've been very careful in deciding what and how to teach; I also know exactly what the instructional goals and objectives are each day. I have collaborated with our special education staff to ensure that each student's Individualized Educational Plan (IEP) includes appropriate instructional goals and objectives that specify exactly how each objective will be taught and measured. The IEPs use the ABCC format: Actor (the student), Behavior (observable/measureable student action), Content (materials/methods used), and Criterion (how student performance will be measured). For example: "Given ten flashcards, John will be able to name ten CVC [consonant-vowel-consonant; e.g., h-a-t] words with 90 percent accuracy."

So this year, it has been so helpful to have Mr. Laird, my special education coteacher, in my classroom for most of the day. Between the two of us, we are able to circulate around the classroom and really monitor and record student learning, as well as respond to any questions or problems students might be having. When we compare our notes, we are able to make accurate decisions about what and how to teach the next day. It's really great because not only are we able to make immediate modifications for any of our students, we can be really smart about planning next steps and ensure that we're adhering to IEPs. We are also really able to "close the loop" between evaluating and planning instruction. (Related tactic is located in Chapter 1: Decide What to Teach under Strategy: Assess to Identify Gaps in Performance.)

Decide What to Teach

Component	Principle	Strategy
Planning Instruction	Decide What to Teach	Assess to Identify Gaps in Performance
		Establish Logical Sequences of Instruction
		Consider Contextual Variables

Chapter 1: Decide What to Teach

Strategy:	**Assess to Identify Gaps in Performance**
Focus:	Basic Skills; Content Skills
Area:	Reading; Mathematics/Problem Solving/Calculating; Writing; Social Studies; Science; Arts; Fitness
Learning Difference:	Attention; Cognition High; Cognition Low; Cognition Mixed; Health; Study Skills; Social Knowledge; Receptive Language/Decoding (listening, reading); Expressive Language/Encoding (speaking, writing, spelling); Fine Motor (handwriting, articulation, etc.); Processing Verbal Information; Processing Visual Information
Disability Category:	Specific Learning Disabilities; Attention Deficit/Hyperactivity Disorder; Visual Impairments; Deafness/Blindness; Gifted and Talented; Hearing Impairments; Mental Retardation; Multiple Disabilities; Traumatic Brain Injury; Second Language Learning Needs; Serious Emotional Disturbance; Speech or Language Impairments; Orthopedic Impairments; Other Health Impairments; Autism

Tactic Title:	**Observing Students**
Problem:	There are times when teachers of students with disabilities evaluate the students and design modifications for their instruction based on the students' assessment test scores. But what do these scores mean? Do these scores allow the teacher to meet the students' needs appropriately?
Tactic:	Direct observation can be used to gain a more comprehensive understanding of the students. While the students are working, walk around the classroom to monitor and record student progress. Ask students questions regarding the lesson and the assignment. Use a checklist to assess desired objectives (see Student Observation Sheet). Write anecdotal records of students' learning, including notes of inappropriate behaviors, underdeveloped thinking skills, on-task behaviors, the understanding of content instruction, or any other noticeable behavior that needs to be documented.
Example:	Observing students as they are working provides a wonderful way for me to monitor their understanding. In fact, I use an Observational Journal to organize my notes during observation. I monitor not only my students' learning, but also their health. The number of days absent or their physical appearance can be a beneficial way of studying their work habits and social skills. (These areas are important to set the framework for the academic learning.) Gathering data through close observation also helps me when collaborating with parents and special education teachers. Parents

and teachers can study my anecdotal records of students showing daily occurrences of behaviors and progress. In this way, decisions concerning the students' education can be made appropriately.

Rosemary T., teacher

Benefits: Measuring learning progress informally can

- confirm other people's observations of the students, the students' test scores, or the students' behaviors;
- help identify and address individual student needs;
- lead to appropriate decisions for students' individualized programs; and
- meet the objectives of a student's Individualized Education Program (IEP).

Literature: Burns, M. S., Delclos, V. R., & Kulewicz, S. J. (1987). Effects of dynamic assessment on teachers' expectations of handicapped children. *American Educational Research Journal, 24,* 325–336.

Student Observation Sheet

Student	Objective(s)	Understanding	Learning Style	Behavior	Comments/Notes

Chapter 1:   Decide What to Teach

Strategy:	**Establish Logical Sequences of Instruction**
Focus:	Basic Skills
Area:	Reading; Mathematics/Problem Solving/Calculating; Writing; Social Studies; Science; Arts; Fitness
Learning Difference:	Attention; Cognition High; Cognition Low; Cognition Mixed; Mobility; Hearing; Health; Memory Short-Term; Memory Long-Term; Seeing; Speaking/Talking; Study Skills; Fine Motor (handwriting, articulation, etc.); Gross Motor (running, walking, etc.); Processing Visual Information; Processing Verbal Information; Receptive Language/Decoding (listening, reading); Expressive Language/Encoding (speaking, writing, spelling); Social Knowledge; Self-Control; Social Behaviors
Disability Category:	Mental Retardation; Specific Learning Disabilities; Multiple Disabilities; Attention Deficit/Hyperactivity Disorder; Visual Impairments; Deafness/Blindness; Gifted and Talented; Traumatic Brain Injury; Hearing Impairments; Second Language Learning Needs; Serious Emotional Disturbance; Speech or Language Impairments; Orthopedic Impairments; Other Health Impairments; Autism

Tactic Title:	**Tailoring Curriculum to Individual Student Needs**
Problem:	Many teachers have difficulty creating a curriculum plan that encompasses the needs of all the students in a classroom. Often, they make changes to accommodate the needs of one student when a broader approach is equally effective.
Tactic:	Design the curriculum in the form of a grid, running objectives vertically and Bloom's taxonomy horizontally (see Curriculum Planner). Place activities in each box.

Bloom's taxonomy organizes cognitive learning into six hierarchical (from lowest to highest) categories:

Level I	**Remembering:** recalling facts, basic concepts, and answers
Level II	**Understanding:** paraphrasing, describing, comparing, interpreting
Level III	**Applying:** solving problems using acquired knowledge in different ways
Level IV	**Analyzing:** breaking information into parts, making inferences, supporting generalizations

Level V   **Evaluating:** making judgments about information, ideas, or quality of work

Level VI   **Creating:** combining elements of information into new patterns or alternatives

Example: I've been a teacher for nine years. I know that, as a general education teacher, I am supposed to include students with disabilities. However, sometimes it is just so hard. I have 23 students and 5 with different types of disabilities: autism, learning disabilities, speech and language impairments, gifted and talented, and hearing impairments. Each one has an Individual Education Plan (IEP) with specific goals and objectives, not to mention the range of abilities among all my other students. I've been working closely with Manuel, my special education coteacher, to develop our grids. We've been using the grids for several months now, and it really has simplified our planning. We also know that we are covering the IEPs.

Kay N., teacher

Benefits: Grid planning is efficient because it

- provides a great way to follow Bloom's taxonomy in everyday practice;
- helps teachers make conscious decisions about the level of thinking they expect from their students by choosing the appropriate level of Bloom's taxonomy;
- incorporates individualized differences;
- allows for higher-order thinking; and
- lays a foundation for knowledge and comprehension.

Literature: Anderson, L. W., & Krathwohl, D. R. (Eds.). (2001). *A taxonomy for learning, teaching, and assessing: A revision of Bloom's taxonomy of educational objectives* (abridged). New York: Longman.

Roberson, T. (1984). Determining curriculum content for the gifted. *Roeper Review, 6,* 137–139.

Curriculum Planner

Instructional Objectives	Bloom's Taxonomy					
	Remembering	Understanding	Applying	Analyzing	Evaluating	Creating
1.						
2.						
3.						
4.						
5.						
6.						

Chapter 1:   Decide What to Teach

Strategy:	**Consider Contextual Variables**

Focus: Basic Skills

Area: Mathematics/Problem Solving/Calculating

Learning Difference: Attention; Expressive Language/Encoding (speaking, writing, spelling); Cognition Mixed; Processing Visual Information

Disability Category: Specific Learning Disabilities

Tactic Title:	**Mathematics in Daily Life**

Problem: Students have difficulties in math because of their inability to read or simply because they do not enjoy it. In other words, variables (differences) in the context (room arrangement, student interest/motivation, instructional arrangements, learning demands, etc.) can have a direct effect on a student's ability to be successful.

Tactic: First, decide on an activity that you know the student will eventually need to use in the future. One example might be an activity in which students are "paid" for the number of hours they are in school. They can then pay their bills with the money they earn. Individuals who plan to work and live independently need to learn this skill. Students can learn to balance their checkbooks every month. If they have extra money, they can use it to "buy" things. This activity continues through the whole year but expands every couple of months. For example, students might have to calculate the tax that is taken out of their checks or decide which kind of car insurance to buy.

Example: I've used this tactic in my classroom; however I "pay" my students with corn kernels. My local camera shop donates empty film containers that my students use to store their kernels. I ask my parents to donate items that we store in a classroom cabinet with glass doors, so the goodies are always visible. Every now and then, we have an "auction" in which students can bid on desired items using their kernels. As the year progresses, the auctions are spaced further apart, and items become more costly. Nevertheless, they are using their mathematical thinking all the time.

Cindy K., teacher

Benefits   Developing a student payment system

- keeps students busy with math and helps them understand its importance;
- helps students see how math is useful in the real world;
- keeps students interested in math; and
- provides a structure for students to build upon prior knowledge as the year goes on.

Literature: Saarimaki, P. (1995). Math in your world. *National Council of Teachers of Mathematics, 9,* 565–569.

Decide How to Teach

Component	Principle	Strategy
Component	*Principle*	*Strategy*
Planning Instruction	Decide How to Teach	Set Instructional Goals
		Establish Performance Standards
		Choose Instructional Methods and Materials
		Establish Grouping Structures
		Pace Instruction Appropriately
		Monitor Performance and Replan Instruction

Chapter 2:   Decide How to Teach

Strategy:	**Set Instructional Goals**
Focus:	Basic Skills
Area:	Reading
Learning Difference:	Attention; Receptive Language/Decoding (listening, reading)
Disability Category:	Mental Retardation; Specific Learning Disabilities; Attention Deficit/ Hyperactivity Disorder; Traumatic Brain Injury; Second Language Learning Needs; Serious Emotional Disturbance; Speech or Language Impairments; Autism

Tactic Title:	**Using Scaffolding to Assist With Reading**
Problem:	Meeting the needs of students with a variety of reading levels in an inclusive classroom can be challenging. Thus, it is essential to set instructional goals that are appropriate for each student.
Tactic:	When developing a reading lesson for an inclusive classroom, consider each student's specific area of need. Then choose a book that will be challenging for both higher- and lower-level readers. Develop several prereading and during-reading activities for the entire class, including one or two activities that can be scaffolded for lower-level readers. Scaffolding activities provide a path for students to move from one learning objective/task to another that is more challenging. In this case, scaffolding activities should provide more detailed information about the book that will provide extra assistance and help them understand the book. Be prepared to spend some extra time explaining these scaffolding activities to the students. Finally, create postreading activities that all students will be able to do. Scaffolding should not be necessary during postreading activities if enough support was given during the prereading and during-reading activities.
Example:	I've used this tactic in my inclusive classroom with great success. I collaborate with my special education colleagues in setting appropriate instructional goals and then choosing the materials and activities that enable all my students to learn. I've even paired my higher- and lower-level readers; this has really helped my struggling readers gain greater independence as learners. Now I understand how important it is to plan prereading, during-reading, and postreading lessons with coinciding activities.
	Jacob T., teacher
Benefits:	By setting instructional goals for individual learning needs, teachers can; • meet the needs of all students in the classroom within one class period; • align their instruction with IEP goals and objectives; and • find opportunities for meaningful collaboration with colleagues.
Literature:	Graves, M., & Graves, B. (1996). Scaffolding reading experiences for inclusive classes. *Educational Leadership, 53*(5), 14–16.

Chapter 2:   Decide How to Teach

Strategy:	**Establish Performance Standards**
Focus:	Basic Skills; Content Skills
Area:	Reading; Mathematics/Problem Solving/Calculating; Writing; Social Studies; Science; Arts; Fitness
Learning Difference:	Receptive Language/Decoding (listening, reading); Expressive Language/Encoding (speaking, writing, spelling); Self-confidence
Disability Category:	Specific Learning Disabilities; Second Language Learning Needs; Speech or Language Impairments

Tactic Title:	**Journal Logs for ESL/EL Students**
Problem:	ESL/EL students often find it difficult to express themselves in English because they are sometimes intimidated by using a second language and struggle for understanding of themselves and their environment.
Tactic:	First, give each student a Journal Log. Then explain the purpose of journals (i.e., thinking on paper; thinking before speaking; "seeing" the language; practicing spelling, grammar, and syntax; and thinking about literary pieces and students' own lives.) Provide students with a prompt (see Journal Prompts) related to reading material. Then demonstrate a response and model the thinking process involved in responding and writing the responses.
Example:	I not only have ESL/EL students who struggle with writing (in English); students with learning disabilities, speech/language impairments, and other disabilities face similar challenges. So I use Journal Logs with all my students. Those who are not able to write using pen/pencil have the option of using the computer to type or dictate their ideas. Others draw pictures and narrate a description to a peer to record.

Alexandra R., teacher

Benefits:	Journal Logs enable students to

- express their ideas without focusing on the mechanics of writing;
- "think before they speak" as they write out their thoughts and ideas;
- "see" the language by recognizing difficult/troubling words and practicing spelling and syntax; and
- develop their cognitive and metacognitive skills as they write reactions to literary pieces.

Literature:	Harris, K. C., & Nevin, A. (1994). Developing and using collaborative bilingual special education teams. In Lilliam M. Malave (Ed.), *Annual Conference Journal, NABE '92–'93* (pp. 25–35). Washington, DC: National Association for Bilingual Education. (ERIC Document Reproduction Service No. ED372643)

Journal Prompts

Reading

I thought the main character in the story should have . . .

I thought the ending . . .

I didn't understand why . . .

I didn't understand how . . .

I really liked . . .

I wish the author had . . .

The illustrations helped me to . . .

This story helped me to . . . because . . .

This story confused me about . . . because . . .

Mathematics

I love . . .

I really need some help understanding . . .

The . . . that my teacher provides help me to . . .

The hardest thing for me is . . . because . . .

I could teach my friends how to . . .

I wish my teacher would . . .

It's really important for me to use a . . . when I am doing math . . . because . . .

. . . is my favorite . . . during math

Other

School is . . .

I am happiest when . . .

It makes me sad when . . .

I wish somebody would . . .

The best thing I ever did was . . .

My family . . .

My friends . . .

After school, I like to . . .

The most amazing thing I have learned is . . .

When I grow up more, I think I want to . . .

Chapter 2:   Decide How to Teach

Strategy:	**Choose Instructional Methods and Materials**
Focus:	Basic Skills
Area:	Reading
Learning Difference:	Attention; Cognition High; Cognition Low; Cognition Mixed; Memory Short-Term; Memory Long-Term; Processing Visual Information; Receptive Language/Decoding (listening, reading)
Disability Category:	Mental Retardation; Specific Learning Disabilities; Multiple Disabilities; Attention Deficit/Hyperactivity Disorder; Visual Impairments; Deafness/Blindness; Gifted and Talented; Traumatic Brain Injury; Hearing Impairments; Second Language Learning Needs; Serious Emotional Disturbance; Speech or Language Impairments; Orthopedic Impairments; Other Health Impairments; Autism
Tactic Title:	**Leveled Reading: Independent Reading**
Problem:	Frequently, students grouped in one classroom read at various grade levels and ability levels. After determining student reading levels, teachers can organize small groups and individual reading assignments based on individual needs. However, choosing a single text becomes difficult, because the teacher knows some students may comprehend it while others cannot. If a text is chosen to suit lower-ability students, others with higher abilities do not improve reading skills.
Tactic:	To enhance all students' reading skills, distribute a Student Interest Survey (see below) to determine the topics that interest each student. Provide an appealing text to each student based on reading level and interest. Finally, provide class time for students to sit quietly and read texts independently. Allow time for students to share and talk about what they are reading with the rest of the class. Another option is to provide students with several personal choices; this approach might be more motivating for some students.
Example:	I really like it when my teacher gives me books about dinosaurs. She knows I like to learn about them and it really helps when there are lots of pictures so I can "see" how they looked and where they lived. Sometimes I read by myself and sometimes I read with José. He reads different books, but that's ok because we can share what we are reading about. He learns about dinosaurs from me and I learn about mammals from him. *Julissa S., student*
Benefits:	Giving students appropriate and personal choices in reading can • increase their ability levels as they gradually conquer each reading grade level;

- boost their self-confidence;
- help them to develop a love for reading;
- bolster student strengths and shore up areas of weakness;
- assist with learning vocabulary and grammar; and
- help them participate in sustained silent reading at their independent reading levels.

Literature: Schirmer, B. R. (1987). Boosting reading success. *Teaching Exceptional Children, 30*(1), 52–55.

Student Interest Survey

Select from among the following to determine your students' interests. Having this information is extremely helpful in designing behavior management plans, determining appropriate consequences for classroom rules, and finding instructional materials and activities that will foster student learning.

I like to . . . , but I really do not like to . . .

Working with others is . . . , but working by myself is . . .

In my free time I . . .

My favorite subject is . . .

I admire . . .

I am afraid of . . .

I am really good at . . .

Books are . . .

Computers are . . .

I know how to . . .

I use computers to . . .

I wish I knew how to . . .

I like to read about . . .

I could teach other people to . . .

I want to know more about . . .

I want to learn how to . . .

I like it when my teacher . . .

I wish my teacher would . . .

I don't like to . . .

I like my best friend because . . .

I wish people would . . .

My favorite time in school is . . .

My favorite time at home is . . .

My family . . .

I wish I could . . .

I wish people knew that I . . .

My favorite animal is . . .

Chapter 2:   Decide How to Teach

Strategy:	**Establish Grouping Structures**
Focus:	Basic Skills
Area:	Reading
Disability Category:	Mental Retardation; Specific Learning Disabilities; Multiple Disabilities; Attention Deficit/Hyperactivity Disorder; Visual Impairments; Deafness/Blindness; Gifted and Talented; Traumatic Brain Injury; Hearing Impairments; Second Language Learning Needs; Serious Emotional Disturbance; Speech or Language Impairments; Orthopedic Impairments; Other Health Impairments; Autism
Learning Difference:	Attention; Mobility; Memory Short-Term; Memory Long-Term; Seeing; Speaking/Talking; Study Skills; Fine Motor (handwriting, articulation, etc.); Gross Motor (running, walking, etc.); Processing Visual Information; Processing Verbal Information; Receptive Language/Decoding (listening, reading); Expressive Language/Encoding (speaking, writing, spelling)
Tactic Title:	**Differentiating Reading Strategies in the Classroom**
Problem:	Teachers often find it difficult to develop a reading lesson that accommodates diverse learners.
Tactic:	To accommodate individual needs, first divide students into four groups. Next assign each group to a different reading center. Assign the first group to the audio center, where they listen to the book. Assign the second group to the teacher, who reads a large-print and picture book with the students. Break the third group into pairs and let them read the book to each other aloud. Let the fourth group work independently in a journal/illustration book about a topic in the story they have been reading. Each group uses the same book for each station. Rotate the membership of each group daily so that all students use all centers and vary the focus of the centers as best meets the needs of students assigned to them (see Center Assignments).
Example:	I love working with Mr. Kim in his classroom. He truly understands how to blend diverse learners and excellent teaching. Together, we've used cooperative learning groups to enable all of our students to be successful, based on their individual needs and abilities. His learning centers provide students with a variety of different learning modes, and his grouping structures blend diverse learners so they can constantly learn from one another. *Shirley H., teacher*

Benefits: Using appropriate grouping structures effectively enables
- students with different learning needs to become better readers or writers or listeners;
- all learners, regardless of ability or learning differences, to participate and succeed with their peers;
- teachers to address the learning needs of all students; and
- teachers to provide individual and/or small-group instruction, based on student needs.

Literature: Shaaban, K. (2006). An initial study of the effects of cooperative learning on reading comprehension, vocabulary acquisition, and motivation to read. *Reading Psychology, 27*, 377–403.

Tomlinson, C. A. (2004). *The differentiated classroom: Responding to the needs of all learners.* Upper Saddle River, NJ: Prentice-Hall.

Center Assignments

Art Center	Audio Center	Teacher Center	Partner Center	Independent Center	Computer Center	_____ Center

Enlarge/Duplicate/Laminate/and post this chart to assign students to various learning centers.

Enter student names (with erasable marker) or tape photographs of students in the appropriate center.

Modifications:

Add/modify columns for content area/time and give to individual students.

Change titles according to content area(s).

Use pictures or symbols with younger students.

Chapter 2:   Decide How to Teach

Strategy:	**Pace Instruction Appropriately**
Focus:	Basic Skills
Area:	Reading; Mathematics/Problem Solving/Calculating; Writing; Social Studies; Science; Arts; Fitness
Learning Difference:	Attention; Cognition Mixed; Study Skills; Fine Motor (handwriting, articulation, etc.); Processing
Disability Category:	Specific Learning Disabilities

Tactic Title:	**Less Is More**
Problem:	Frequently students with disabilities cannot complete similar quantities of work in the same time frame as their peers. Some students just need more time to read and understand the material.
Tactic:	Establish realistic expectations for individual learning needs. Next adjust the activities and materials to meet the needs of students. For example, during a math lesson, students with disabilities can complete modified worksheets. While students without disabilities may complete 50 math problems in a set period, students with learning disabilities may complete fewer problems in the same period.
Example:	I've always believed that it is important to teach my students that differences in our learning are the norm. Therefore, students in my classroom know that not everyone's tasks will be the same, and they share responsibility for one another's learning. Not only do I adjust the quantity of learning tasks, I also provide different time frames for completing assignments. I found that some students give up on assignments because they see other students finishing before them and they begin to have feelings of failure. Giving these students an assignment that requires less work yet still provides a valuable learning experience is great. Works for me. Works for my students. *Albert R., teacher*
Benefits:	Pacing instruction appropriately • applies to all subject areas and disabilities; • enables students with disabilities to have their individual needs met in a variety of content areas; • prevents students from rushing through their work, only giving it half their effort in the hope that they will finish on time; and • enables teachers to be more successful with a variety of learners.
Literature:	Niebling, B. C., & Elliott, S. N. (2005). Testing accommodations and inclusive assessment practices. *Assessment for Effective Intervention, 31*(1), 1–6.

Chapter 2:   Decide How to Teach

Strategy:	**Monitor Performance and Replan Instruction**
Focus:	Basic Skills
Area:	Reading
Learning Difference:	Attention; Cognition Low; Processing Visual Information; Receptive Language/Decoding (listening, reading); Processing Verbal Information
Disability Category:	Specific Learning Disabilities; Mental Retardation; Visual Impairments; Speech or Language Impairments; Second Language Learning Needs; Autism; Attention Deficit/Hyperactivity Disorder

Tactic Title:	**Building Self-Confidence in Struggling Readers**
Problem:	Many students who struggle with reading become frustrated with repeated failure. This can lead to a lack of motivation and result in failure to learn.
Tactic:	Identify the reading level of the student. Provide books that are on a lower level so that student can gain self-confidence in reading. Have the student read the book silently and then fill out a Story Map (see below), identifying the main characters, setting, main events, problems, and conclusion/outcome. Review the story map to see if the student has gained any greater insight into the story. Once confident that the student has mastered that reading level, raise the difficulty level of the books being read. Repeat the same routine for each book. If the student becomes discouraged at any point in the process, provide the student with an easier book that the student will be able to read confidently. Give continuous positive and supportive/corrective feedback.
Example:	I've found that this tactic allows my struggling readers, regardless of ability or disability, to be challenged continuously while improving their reading and listening skills. Furthermore, because they are able to move to easier reading levels from time to time, they are less discouraged and more focused on the positive aspects of learning. I know that it is important to provide positive feedback, and having students read aloud helps me do so. Once a student has mastered the decoding process and has acquired the skills necessary to read independently, silent reading is possible.

Holly I., teacher

Benefits:	Daily monitoring of student performance enables teachers to

- replan instruction based on student performance on a day-to-day basis;
- provide appropriate learning opportunities;
- apply this tactic across all content and disability areas; and
- provide accurate/current information to special educators, parents, and the student.

Literature:	Duffy-Hester, A. (1999). Teaching struggling readers in elementary school classrooms: A review of classroom reading programs and principles for instruction. *The Reading Teacher, 52,* 480–495.

Story Map

Name _____   **Date** _____

Title: _____

    Author: _____

    Illustrator: _____

    Publisher/Date: _____

Main Characters:

Setting:

Main Events:

Problems:

Conclusion/Outcome:

3

Communicate Realistic Expectations

Component	Principle	Strategy
Planning Instruction	Communicate Realistic Expectations	Teach Goals, Objectives, and Standards
		Teach Students to Be Active, Involved Learners
		Teach Students Consequences of Performance

Chapter 3:   Communicate Realistic Expectations

Strategy:	**Teach Goals, Objectives, and Standards**
Focus:	Basic Skills
Area:	Reading; Mathematics/Problem Solving/Calculating; Writing; Social Studies; Science; Arts; Fitness
Learning Difference:	Attention; Memory Short-Term; Processing Verbal Information; Self-Control; Social Behaviors; Social Knowledge
Disability Category:	Multiple Disabilities

Tactic Title:	**Clarifying Expectations to Maintain a Productive Learning Environment**
Problem:	Students are more successful when they know what is expected of them.
Tactic:	First, tell students the instructional goals, learning objectives, and performance standards prior to beginning any instruction. These can be posted and/or provided in their individual packets (see Posting Expectations). Discuss your academic expectations with students; check for understanding. Focus on the positive results and tell students how to achieve them.
Example:	I am a special education teacher, and I coteach with Ms. Laub every morning. We use our common planning time to lay out several days of instruction. It is really helpful to have everyone "on the same page" regarding instructional goals, learning objectives, and standards. This doesn't mean that everyone is doing exactly the same activity. We make accommodations for individual students and small groups of students, so we can address the goals and objectives of IEPs too. I'm always very careful to ask students what they think the expectations are and how they are going to meet them.
	Rene Z., teacher
Benefits:	Teaching students what is expected of them <ul><li>is an excellent way to minimize disruptions in a positive learning environment;</li><li>teaches students that differences in learning are the norm; and</li><li>provides a structure for their learning and helps them understand why the expectations are important.</li></ul>
Literature:	Mayer, G. R. (1999). Constructive discipline for school personnel. *Education and Treatment of Children, 22,* 36–54.

Posting Expectations

Use/Modify this form to inform students of your expectations and maintain documentation. Post for large and/or small groups; provide individualized/modified versions for students with disabilities. Inserting names/dates/activity information might be appropriate in some cases.

Instructional Goal(s):

Learning Objective(s):

Performance Standard(s):

Related IEP Goals/Objectives/Benchmarks:

Related Standards:

Chapter 3: Communicate Realistic Expectations

Strategy:	**Teach Students to Be Active, Involved Learners**
Focus:	Basic Skills
Area:	Reading
Learning Difference:	Processing Visual Information; Receptive Language/Decoding (listening, reading)
Disability Category:	Specific Learning Disabilities; Traumatic Brain Injury

Tactic Title:	**Competitive Reading**
Problem:	Many students with disabilities face difficulties in reading at their grade level, particularly those with specific learning disabilities or traumatic brain injury.
Tactic:	Give students a packet (see Timed Reading Sheets) with approximately 200 words that have a common trait, such as having only one syllable or beginning with th and sh. The students, one at a time, then are timed on how many words they can read in a minute. Their results are recorded on their individual charts, which will show their progress and what they need to work on. As a student's reading level improves, more complex words, short sentences, and finally books can be used.
Example:	I really like racing words with Xavier. Every morning, we go to the reading center to get our reading lists. We have the same words, but they are not in the same order. Then, I start the timer and read as many words as fast as I can in one minute. Xavier checks off the words that I read correctly; then we switch. When we're done, we count the checkmarks to see how many we did correctly and record our scores on our chart. Mr. Thomas also lets us tape our reading, so he can check later. I used to only read about 15 words in a minute; now, I can read about 40 . . . so, I'm getting better. Sometimes, we use the Language Master to practice our trouble words. I think Mr. Thomas is going to give me a new list in a few days.

Jasmine C., student |
| *Benefits:* | Competition
• is most effective when students are at similar levels;
• can improve students' speed in word recognition, number facts, and other areas where recall is important;
• gives the teacher ongoing data regarding the students' levels; |

- makes learning fun without the pressure students may naturally feel; and
- ensures that everyone succeeds, thus potentially improving their self-efficacy.

Literature: Bolocofsky, D. N. (1980). Motivational effects of classroom competition as a function of field dependence. *Journal of Educational Research, 73,* 213–217.

Timed Reading Sheet

1			51			101			151	
2			52			102			152	
3			53			103			153	
4			54			104			154	
5			55			105			155	
6			56			106			156	
7			57			107			157	
8			58			108			158	
9			59			109			159	
10			60			110			160	
11			61			111			161	
12			62			112			162	
13			63			113			163	
14			64			114			164	
15			65			115			165	
16			66			116			166	
17			67			117			167	
18			68			118			168	
19			69			119			169	
20			70			120			170	
21			71			121			171	
22			72			122			172	
23			73			123			173	
24			74			124			174	
25			75			125			175	
26			76			126			176	
27			77			127			177	
28			78			128			178	
29			79			129			179	
30			80			130			180	
31			81			131			181	
32			82			132			182	
33			83			133			183	
34			84			134			184	
35			85			135			185	
36			86			136			186	
37			87			137			187	
38			88			138			188	
39			89			139			189	
40			90			140			190	
41			91			141			191	
42			92			142			192	
43			93			143			193	
44			94			144			194	
45			95			145			195	
46			96			146			196	
47			97			147			197	
48			98			148			198	
49			99			149			199	
50			100			150			200	

Reading Rates

Student Name: _____

Visual Analysis: Plot Dates and Rates Below
Plot

Date	Rate

# of Words

Date

Chapter 3: Communicate Realistic Expectations

Strategy:	**Teach Students Consequences of Performance**
Focus:	Basic Skills
Area:	Reading; Mathematics/Problem Solving/Calculating; Writing; Social Studies; Science; Arts; Fitness
Learning Difference:	Attention; Seeing; Mobility; Speaking/Talking; Cognition High; Cognition Low; Cognition Mixed; Hearing; Health; Fine Motor (handwriting, articulation, etc.); Expressive Language/Encoding (speaking, writing, spelling); Receptive Language/Decoding (listening, reading); Memory Long-Term; Memory Short-Term; Processing Visual Information; Processing Verbal Information; Study Skills; Social Knowledge; Self-Control; Social Behaviors; Self-Confidence
Disability Category:	Multiple Disabilities; Specific Learning Disabilities; Speech or Language Impairments; Gifted and Talented; Attention Deficit/Hyperactivity Disorder; Visual Impairments; Deafness/Blindness; Hearing Impairments; Mental Retardation; Traumatic Brain Injury; Second Language Learning Needs; Serious Emotional Disturbance; Orthopedic Impairments; Other Health Impairments; Autism

Tactic Title:	**Using Peers to Enhance Understanding of Assignments**
Problem:	Students who are very capable of learning may lack motivation or understanding to complete learning activities. They need assistance in understanding the positive consequences of performing successfully.
Tactic:	Develop a signal (e.g., hand raising, displaying a "help" sign) that students can use to indicate the need for help with an assignment. Offer groups of students the privilege of being peer tutors to the other students upon satisfactory completion of the assigned task.
Example:	I've always liked using peer tutoring with my students because it is so adaptable across students, content areas, and activities. I do take time to teach how to be a tutor; in fact, tutors use a checklist to be sure they follow the steps in sequence. For example:

1. Check for tutee's understanding of the task.
2. Review tutee's progress.
3. Ask the tutee to describe the problem.
4. Provide assistance in small steps.
5. Encourage the tutee to "take over" whenever it is appropriate.

I also teach tutees appropriate behavior:

1. Use prearranged signal.
2. Wait quietly (try another problem, read a book, etc.).
3. Describe the task.

4. Listen carefully.
5. Try again.
6. Thank your tutor.

I make sure that every student gets an opportunity to be a tutor. This really encourages learning and teaches students the consequences of meeting learning expectations.

Matt K., teacher

Benefits: Using peers in this way

- models appropriate task completion;
- uses peer tutoring as the consequence of learning;
- engages all learners productively, while decreasing classroom distraction levels; and
- encourages capable students to complete their work so they can receive the social rewards of being a tutor.

Literature: Kroeger, S. D., & Kouche, B. (2006). Using peer-assisted learning strategies to increase response to intervention in inclusive middle math settings. *Teaching Exceptional Children, 38*(5), 6–13.

PART II

Managing Instruction

Effective teachers manage their instruction by preparing classrooms and learning materials to maximize the success of their students, by using instructional time productively, and by making classrooms positive learning environments. In this part of our resource, we describe evidence-based strategies for each principle of managing instruction.

Component	Principle	Strategy
Managing Instruction (Part II)	Prepare for Instruction (Chapter 4)	Set Classroom Rules
		Communicate and Teach Classroom Rules
		Communicate Consequences of Behavior
		Handle Disruptions Efficiently
		Teach Students to Manage Their Own Behavior
	Use Time Productively (Chapter 5)	Establish Routines and Procedures
		Organize Physical Space
		Allocate Sufficient Time to Academic Activities
	Establish Positive Classroom Environment (Chapter 6)	Make the Classroom a Pleasant, Friendly Place
		Accept Individual Differences
		Establish Supportive, Cooperative Learning Environments
		Create a Nonthreatening Learning Environment

Managing Instruction Works: A Case Study

As a new teacher, I quickly learned the importance of consistency and structure in a classroom. I started over ten years ago as a kindergarten teacher, and, of course, I wanted my classroom to be perfect, so I kept changing schedules and rearranging the learning centers. I also put every game, puzzle, manipulative, and Letter Person, aka "huggable" (Alphatime Reading Program) out so my students could use them. Big mistake. A recipe for chaos and lost instructional time. The final straw came when I got a haircut over the weekend. When we started the day on Monday, I quickly realized there was a problem. When I asked what was wrong, one my students said: "We want the old Ms. Cooper back." So I learned a very important lesson. Learners, especially young learners and those with disabilities, really need things to be reliable and predictable. Changes need to be taught carefully. So I learned the hard way to establish routines and procedures and keep them consistent; also, I'm much more knowledgeable as to how to organize and, on occasion, reorganize the physical space in my classroom. (Related tactics are located in Chapter 5: Use Time Productively under Strategy: Establish Routines and Procedures and Strategy: Organize Physical Space.)

Prepare for Instruction

Component	Principle	Strategy
Managing Instruction	Prepare for Instruction	Set Classroom Rules
		Communicate and Teach Classroom Rules
		Communicate Consequences of Behavior
		Handle Disruptions Efficiently
		Teach Students to Manage Their Own Behavior

Chapter 4:   Prepare for Instruction

Strategy:	**Set Classroom Rules**

Focus:	Basic Skills
Area:	Reading; Mathematics/Problem Solving/Calculating; Writing; Social Studies; Science
Learning Difference:	Social Knowledge; Self-Control; Social Behaviors; Self-Confidence; Self-Care
Disability Category:	Attention Deficit/Hyperactivity Disorder; Serious Emotional Disturbance

Tactic Title:	**The Democratic Classroom**

Problem:	Many teachers have difficulty enforcing rules in their classrooms. As a result, many resort to authoritarian teaching styles and use punishment when dealing with negative behavior.
Tactic:	Students are more respectful of rules and regulations when they help to create the basic principles that comprise their classroom constitution. Involve students in determining the essential rules of their classroom. Only three to five rules are needed. State rules positively so they tell students what to do, rather than what not to do. For example, "Walk," rather than, "Don't run"; "Listen," rather than, "Don't talk out." Require students to develop consequences for following and not following the rules (see Classroom Rules).
Example:	One of the very first things I do on the first day of school is to have a class meeting to determine the classroom rules, although we call them "Principles." I ask the students for their ideas, but I am sure to incorporate mine as well. I might propose a "problem," such as "How do you feel when someone pushes you?" or "You know, I was watching all of the students on the playground before school, and I saw Ronaldo running on the blacktop. Then, he fell and scraped his knee. He was crying and had to go to the Nurse's office. Why do you think that happened?" The discussion that follows leads to positively stated principles, such as "Keep my hands to myself," or "Walk." Sometimes, we have a discussion as to what some of the words mean: *kind, respect, tolerance,* etc. Then, we write the principles down:

We promise to

> walk;
> keep our hands to ourselves; and
> be kind.

And everyone, including me, my paraprofessionals, and my special education coteacher, signs our names.

Then, we post the Principles on the wall.

We also develop a three-stage "warning and consequence system":

1. Silent cue/reminder
2. Verbal reminder
3. Phone call home

When they go through this process, students are forced to consider other people's feelings. Therefore, they create rules that they believe are fair and reasonable.

Katie T., teacher

Benefits:

When students are involved in determining classroom rules and consequences, they

- can follow the rules and also understand the reasons behind these rules;
- take greater ownership; and
- increase their self-efficacy, self-discipline, and social responsibility.

Literature:

Willis, S. (1996). Managing today's classroom: Finding Alternatives to Control and Compliance. *Education Update (Newsletter of the Association for Supervision and Curriculum Development), 38*(6), 1, 3–7.

Classroom Rules

Use this form as a template for developing, posting, and individualizing rules for students in your class-room. There is space at the bottom for students to "sign" their agreement with the class's constitution. Thus, when posted, this becomes a useful reminder for those who might find the rules challenging at times. Simply "pointing" out the consequences is a very effective nonverbal tool.

Rule	Positive Consequences	Negative Consequences

Chapter 4: Prepare for Instruction

Strategy:	**Communicate and Teach Classroom Rules**
Focus:	Basic Skills
Area:	Reading; Mathematics/Problem Solving/Calculating; Writing; Social Studies; Science
Learning Difference:	Attention; Self-Control; Social Behaviors
Disability Category:	Attention Deficit/Hyperactivity Disorder; Attention Deficit Disorder; Serious Emotional Disturbance

Tactic Title:	**Personal Signals for Inappropriate Classroom Behavior**
Problem:	Frequently, students with ADD/ADHD or behavioral issues act inappropriately on impulse. This can disrupt their own learning and that of other students.
Tactic:	Meet with the student privately and individually. Explain that you enjoy the student's participation in class activities but that you can see that the student is struggling with one or two of the class rules. Tell the student you want to devise a personal signal as a reminder to work on self-control. Next, allow the student to choose from a few options. One option could be that the teacher will casually tap a pen on the corner of the student's desk when passing by. This is most discrete if the teacher frequently roams around the room. Finally, try it out for a week and meet again with the student to decide on its effectiveness.
Example:	My teacher and I have a secret code to help me stay on task. We figured it out together. . . . When he touches the top of his head, it means I need to focus on what I'm supposed to be doing. He says that he is "thanking his brain" to remind it to keep learning . . . so, that's what I do too! I like it that he is paying attention to me and trying to help me. . . . Makes me feel that he is on my side.
	Isaiah G., student
Benefits:	Using private signals to inform students about their behavior • enables them to be a part of the decision-making process; • helps them to manage their behavior; • is appropriate for students at almost any grade level; and • is an effective way to inform a student about inappropriate behavior without interrupting others.
Literature:	Epstein, T., & Elias, M. (1996). To reach for the stars: How social/affective education can foster truly inclusive environments. *Phi Delta Kappan, 78,* 157–163.

Chapter 4:   Prepare for Instruction

Strategy:	**Communicate Consequences of Behavior**
Focus:	Basic Skills
Area:	Reading; Mathematics/Problem Solving/Calculating; Writing; Social Studies; Science; Arts; Fitness
Learning Difference:	Cognition High; Cognition Low; Cognition Mixed; Attention; Study Skills; Self-Control; Social Behaviors; Processing Verbal Information; Self-Confidence
Disability Category:	Attention Deficit/Hyperactivity Disorder; Traumatic Brain Injury; Second Language Learning Needs; Serious Emotional Disturbance; Specific Learning Disabilities; Speech or Language Impairments; Autism

Tactic Title:	**Accenting the Positive**
Problem:	Students often have difficulty paying attention, staying on-task, and responding to teacher expectations and directions.
Tactic:	Clarify expectations and provide directions in positive ways that tell students what to do instead of what not to do. State consequences in a positive way and avoid threats. For example, tell students, "When you put on your shoes, you can go to the nurse," rather than, "If you do not put on your shoes, you cannot go to the nurse." Allow students to make decisions regarding their behavior (e.g., "If you complete this task, you may hold your water bottle."). In this way, students know the positive consequences of appropriate behavior, feel more secure, and have some control over their behavior.
Example:	I like focusing on the positive outcomes . . . makes my classroom a much happier place to be. I'd never tell a student, "Go read," but so often, teachers will say things like, "Behave; you know what to do," when, in fact, the student doesn't know exactly what is expected. So my supportive correction always includes what the student is to do in order to achieve the positive consequences. "When you finish your activity, you may . . ." "When you return to your seat, I will . . ." "When you walk, you may . . ." *Dustin R., teacher*
Benefits:	Teaching students the consequences of their behavior in positive ways • meets the needs of the students and the teacher's expectations at the same time; • works well with all students in the classroom; and • teaches students what to do, rather than focusing on what not to do.
Literature:	Dowd, J. (1997). Refusing to play the blame game. *Educational Leadership, 54,* 67–69.

Chapter 4: Prepare for Instruction

Strategy:	**Handle Disruptions Efficiently**
Focus:	Basic Skills
Area:	Reading; Mathematics/Problem Solving/Calculating; Writing; Social Studies; Science; Arts; Fitness
Learning Difference:	Attention; Social Knowledge; Self-Control; Social Behaviors; Self-Confidence
Disability Category:	Attention Deficit/Hyperactivity Disorder

Tactic Title:	**Nonverbal Promotion of On-Task Behavior**
Problem	It is often frustrating when students with Attention Deficit/ Hyperactivity Disorder (ADHD) act out inappropriately in class. Some examples of acting out include shouting answers, being overly excited, and distracting fellow classmates with incessant talking.
Tactic:	First, when the student acts out in an inappropriate way, give a discrete but serious nonverbal facial expression while continuing to conduct the class. If required, use hand movements and nonverbal facial expressions that signal the student to stop or settle down. If the student continues to act inappropriately, walk by or stand next to the student to acknowledge the student's disruption. Use a simple chart (see the Behavior Chart) to keep track of progress.
Example:	I like using this tactic because it doesn't take time away from teaching or learning. I can meet the needs of different students and help them learn how to manage their own behavior. Also, I am not creating "more noise" by trying to be heard above the level of the disruption. Sometimes when the gesture or eye contact don't seem to be working, I pass by the student's desk and put a checkmark on the behavior chart that is taped to the desk. . . . I can always erase it later if behavior improves. . . . The behavior chart also has spaces for recognizing positive/appropriate behavior. Eventually, I'll let the students fill in the chart themselves. *Lori N., teacher*
Benefits:	Using nonverbal cues • manages student behavior without being intrusive to the learning environment; • helps students learn to modify their own behavior; • can be individualized for different students; and • is not disruptive to others.
Literature:	Sprouse, C. A., Hall, C. W., Webster, R. E., & Bolen, L. M. (1998). Social perception in students with learning disabilities and attention deficit/ hyperactivity disorder. *Journal of Nonverbal Behavior, 22,* 125–134.

Behavior Chart

Name _____   Date _____

Target Behavior: _____

Time	Yes	No
Total:		

Chapter 4:   Prepare for Instruction

Strategy:	**Teach Students to Manage Their Own Behavior**
Focus:	Basic Skills
Area:	Reading; Mathematics/Problem Solving/Calculating; Writing; Social Studies; Science; Arts; Fitness
Learning Difference:	Attention; Cognition Mixed; Social Knowledge; Self-Control; Social Behaviors; Self-Confidence
Disability Category:	Attention Deficit/Hyperactivity Disorder; Serious Emotional Disturbance

Tactic Title:	**Sticker Reward Chart**
Problem:	Frequently, students with ADD/ADHD have difficulty staying on-task. Teachers often find that these students need one-on-one attention and reinforcement.
Tactic:	Create a chart (see Sticker Reward Chart and Rewarding Behavior Template) for the student that divides each day into four parts. If the student gets through a part of the day successfully, give the student a sticker. Then, as behavior improves, students decide with the teacher if they should get a sticker. If at the end of the day, the student has received four stickers, give a predetermined and appropriate award. Use a Rewarding Behavior template (see page 45) to create other charts for monitoring and rewarding behavior.
Example:	I like monitoring student behavior throughout the day . . . helps keep all of us on track and focusing on the positive. I use a combination of responsive classroom techniques (reinforcing, reminding, and redirecting) together with the charts to help my students recognize their own inappropriate behavior. I have found that, after a while, I can reduce the number of recordings during the day and gradually shift to more "natural" reinforcers, such as checkmarks, praise, or a learning activity that the student wants. It is so important to involve students in the process of monitoring and managing their own behavior—an essential lifelong skill. Students can also bring their charts home and show their parents how well they are doing in school. It's nice when I can send home "good news."

Jim K., teacher

Benefits:	Teaching students to manage their own behavior
	• works with all students and behaviors;
	• gives them responsibility and control;

- can improve their self-efficacy; and
- can be used in other classes and at home.

Literature:

Charney, R. S. (2002). *Teaching children to care: Classroom management for ethical and academic growth, K–8* (rev. ed.). Turners Falls, MA: Northeast Foundation for Children.

Ruth, W. J. (1996). Goal setting and behavior contracting for students with emotional and behavioral difficulties. *Psychology in the Schools, 33,* 153–158.

Sticker Reward Chart

Time	Monday	Tuesday	Wednesday	Thursday	Friday
9–10:30					
10:30–11					
11–12:30					
12:30–2					

What I am working for is

_____

Rewarding Behavior Template

Name _____   Date_____

Target Behavior: _____

Time Period	Yes	No

5

Use Time Productively

Component	Principle	Strategy
Managing Instruction	Use Time Productively	Establish Routines and Procedures
		Organize Physical Space
		Allocate Sufficient Time to Academic Activities

Chapter 5:   Use Time Productively

Strategy:	**Establish Routines and Procedures**
Focus:	Basic Skills
Area:	Reading; Mathematics/Problem Solving/Calculating; Writing; Social Studies; Science; Arts; Fitness
Learning Difference:	Attention; Self-Control; Social Behaviors; Self-Confidence
Disability Category:	Attention Deficit/Hyperactivity Disorder

Tactic Title:	**Increasing On-Task Behavior for Students With ADHD**
Problem:	Teachers can implement strategies in their classrooms that will increase a student's on-task time, academic performance, and positive interactions with peers.
Tactic:	Establish structure in the classroom by regularly reviewing the daily schedule and the classroom rules. Review expectations frequently. Arrange the classroom so that the student with ADHD can have a desk closer to the teacher or a peer. Present lessons using visual aids, such as videos and posters. Respond to inappropriate behaviors immediately after they occur. Use contingencies to reinforce appropriate behaviors. Teach students to monitor their own behavior.
Example:	I have several students in my class who have benefited from this strategy . . . not just Diego who has ADHD. I find that most students really like structure and routines. Reviewing the routines, procedures, and the daily schedule provides my students with a sense of safety and also self-confidence, because they know what to expect. Seating students strategically is also important . . . especially when they can take advantage of appropriate role models. *Angie T., teacher*
Benefits:	Establishing structure, routines, and procedures • allows students to be more focused and directed; • can encourage positive interaction among students; • benefits all students; and • makes it easy for teachers to use proximity control.
Literature:	Levy, N. R. (1996). Classroom strategies for managing students with attention-deficit/hyperactivity disorder. *Intervention in School and Clinic, 32*(2), 89–94.

Chapter 5:   Use Time Productively

Strategy:	**Organize Physical Space**
Focus:	Basic Skills
Area:	Reading; Mathematics/Problem Solving/Calculating; Writing; Social Studies; Science
Learning Difference:	Attention; Social Behaviors
Disability Category:	Attention Deficit/Hyperactivity Disorder

Tactic Title:	**Using Seating Arrangements to Everyone's Advantage**
Problem:	Many students have difficulty staying on-task during group work because they cannot communicate effectively with one another.
Tactic:	The desks in many classrooms are arranged in rows, and the arrangement does not change for different activities. During group work, some group members are often left out, and many students do not benefit from the activity. When appropriate, change the arrangement of the desks in the room prior to group lessons. The desks should be arranged in groups of three or four. As students enter the room, they will know that a group activity is planned. With the new seating arrangement, students can interact with each other more easily, and the quality of work will most likely improve.
Example:	I've found that when I am giving instructions or previewing the day, it is much easier for my students to focus if they are arranged in rows (even sitting on the floor) where there are fewer opportunities for interaction with each other. Then, once they understand the routine or activity, they move to areas of the room where they can interact in small groups or work independently. I really don't have to move much furniture on a day-to-day basis, as I have tables and clusters of desks, learning centers, and study carrels in place. *Sophia Y., teacher*
Benefits:	When appropriate group arrangements are used, • the quality of student work improves; • teachers spend less time addressing off-task behavior; • there is more time to address subject-specific questions; • students learn to work together productively and appropriately in a social and intellectual setting; and • teachers can differentiate instruction according to individual needs.
Literature:	Bonus, M., & Riordan, L. (1998). *Increasing student on-task behavior through the use of specific seating arrangements* (Master's Action Research Project). Chicago: Saint Xavier University. (ERIC Document Reproduction Service No. ED422129) Campbell, P., & Siperstein, G. N. (1994). *Improving social competence: A resource for elementary school teachers.* Boston: Allyn & Bacon.

Chapter 5:   Use Time Productively

Strategy:	**Allocate Sufficient Time to Academic Activities**
Focus:	Basic Skills
Area:	Reading; Mathematics/Problem Solving/Calculating; Writing; Social Studies; Science
Learning Difference:	Attention; Memory Short-Term; Memory Long-Term; Study Skills
Disability Category:	Mental Retardation; Specific Learning Disabilities; Attention Deficit/ Hyperactivity Disorder; Second Language Learning Needs; Serious Emotional Disturbance; Autism

Tactic Title:	**Increasing Academic Learning Time: Using Homework Effectively**
Problem:	Students often have difficulty remembering and completing homework assignments.
Tactic:	The appropriate use of homework can increase academic learning time significantly. Give students a sheet for recording homework assignments (see Homework Assignments). Teach students to record homework assignments accurately in their notebooks. Ensure that the assignment is appropriate for independent practice. Students should be able to complete assignments on their own because they are working on proficiency, not the acquisition of new knowledge. Ensure that students understand the assignment. Require parent signatures each evening, even if there are no assignments. Then, each morning, verify that homework has been completed.
Example:	Homework notebooks/weekly planners are a wonderful tool for giving my students extra opportunities to practice and refine their skills. I'm always careful to give them assignments that are meaningful and can be completed independently . . . when they are at the proficiency level. Homework is not a time for practicing errors . . . so, I never give homework that asks them to practice newly acquired information. The notebooks also create a way for me to have ongoing communication with parents and caregivers. I've even included spaces for the academic calendar, classroom newsletters, behavior charts, special announcements, and personal notes. Parents really seem to like them, and I find that my students are completing their homework more accurately. *Jennifer S., teacher*
Benefits:	When homework notebooks are used appropriately; • students learn to take responsibility for remembering and completing homework; • they can be applied to all subject areas and grade levels; and • academic learning time is increased.
Literature:	Stormont-Spurgin, M. (1997). I lost my homework: Strategies for improving organization in students with ADHD. *Intervention in School and Clinic, 32,* 270–274.

Homework Assignments

Date Assigned	Assignment	Date Due	Signature	Date

6

Establish Positive Classroom Environment

Component	Principle	Strategy
Managing Instruction	Establish Positive Classroom Environment	Make the Classroom a Pleasant, Friendly Place
		Accept Individual Differences
		Establish Supportive, Cooperative Learning Environments
		Create a Nonthreatening Learning Environment

Chapter 6:   Establish Positive Classroom Environment

Strategy:	**Make the Classroom a Pleasant, Friendly Place**
Focus:	Basic Skills
Area:	Reading; Mathematics/Problem Solving/Calculating; Writing; Social Studies; Science; Arts; Fitness
Learning Difference:	Speaking/Talking; Expressive Language/Encoding (speaking, writing, spelling); Social Behaviors
Disability Category:	Autism

Tactic Title:	**Helping Students With Autism to Cope in the Classroom**
Problem:	Students with autism generally have a difficult time adjusting to classroom routines.
Tactic:	Find an activity that the student enjoys and engages in willingly. Lunch often works very well. Then use that activity to reinforce acceptable behavior. For example, students who enjoy lunch verbalize the most at that time because they must use words to have a teacher open their milk or a bag of chips. Start simply, teaching the student a word at a time. "More" will work at first, but as the student becomes more comfortable and trusting, withhold the item until the student requests, "More milk, please."
Example:	The "classroom" is anywhere students have an opportunity to learn— the typical classroom, lunch, recess, physical education, walking in the hallways. I've learned to take advantage of learning opportunities and make those places/situations/opportunities as safe and pleasant as possible. I know my students learn when they feel welcome and know they are among friends . . . even if it is a "tall person." *Carla J., teacher*
Benefits:	Creating safe and pleasant "classrooms," wherever they may be, • lets teachers use an enjoyable activity that helps students remain focused and calm; • helps students to learn to trust over time; and • can engage all educators in a student's day.
Literature:	Macy, M. G., & Bricker, D. D. (2007). Embedding individualized social goals into routine activities in inclusive early childhood classrooms. *Early Child Development & Care, 177,* 107–120.

Chapter 6: Establish Positive Classroom Environment

Strategy:	**Accept Individual Differences**
Focus:	Basic Skills
Area:	Reading; Mathematics/Problem Solving/Calculating; Writing; Social Studies; Science; Arts; Fitness
Learning Difference:	Cognition Low; Study Skills; Fine Motor (handwriting, articulation, etc.); Receptive Language/Decoding (listening, reading); Expressive Language/Encoding (speaking, writing, spelling); Self-Control; Social Behaviors
Disability Category:	Mental Retardation

Tactic Title:	**Introduction and Expectations Regarding New Students**
Problem:	Students exhibiting the characteristic behaviors consistent with mental retardation or other disability often have difficulty adjusting to a new classroom. Because these students often have underdeveloped social skills, it is difficult for them to relate to the other students and to express their needs and wants.
Tactic:	Explain some characteristics of the new student's behaviors to the class prior to the student being brought into the classroom. Relate these behaviors to some of the daily activities. Explain to the other students in the class their roles in welcoming and assisting the student. Students may have signed a class contract at the beginning of the year, which would make this easier. Remind everyone that the only person who has the right to "put someone down" is a perfect person, and there are no perfect people.
Example:	Last year, Lucinda joined our class. Lucinda was born with spina bifida and used crutches and a wheelchair. Before she arrived, my paraprofessional, the school nurse, her special education teachers, and I talked with my students about spina bifida. When Lucinda arrived, each of my students presented her with a personal welcome. Her wonderful mom stayed and talked about Luci and shared her hopes with us. A few weeks later, Luci let my students use her wheelchair and try on her leg braces. Luci truly transformed our classroom.
	Jerry R., teacher
Benefits:	Teaching all students that differences are a part of life in the classroom
	• enables students to take responsibility for accepting others;
	• gives students ownership of their responsibilities to their classmates;
	• fosters community and class pride in behavior; and
	• applies to all grade levels, learning differences, and disabilities.
Literature:	Murphy, D. M. (1996). Implications of inclusion for general and special education. *The Elementary School Journal, 96,* 469–493.

Chapter 6:   Establish Positive Classroom Environment

Strategy:	**Establish Supportive, Cooperative Learning Environments**
Focus:	Basic Skills
Area:	Reading; Mathematics/Problem Solving/Calculating; Writing; Social Studies; Arts; Fitness
Learning Difference:	Speaking/Talking; Processing Visual Information; Processing Verbal Information; Receptive Language/Decoding (listening, reading); Expressive Language/Encoding (speaking, writing, spelling); Self-Confidence
Disability Category:	Specific Learning Disabilities; Speech or Language Impairments

Tactic Title:	**Encouraging Verbal Involvement**
Problem:	Students with learning disabilities often have low self-esteem due to their challenges in processing language. Consequently, they sometimes feel uncomfortable sharing their work with others.
Tactic:	Verbal involvement by those with language processing disorders should be encouraged. Seek out opportunities for students to share their work or ideas. Some may excel at written work; others shine verbally. If a student with special needs, such as a writing deficiency, wants to contribute to class discussions about their ideas, ensure that this student is given a chance to share.
Example:	My teacher, Mr. Pierce, is really good about making me look good. He knows I have trouble with writing; he also knows that I have pretty good ideas in my head and I can talk about them really well. So, when we have our Writer's Workshop, where we share our writing . . . he just lets me talk about my work and I feel really good about that. He never *makes* me share my writing, unless I want to. Then he helps me with the writing part himself. Last week, I was "Star of the Week" in writing; my dad was so proud. Mr. Pierce is a really great teacher. *Nya P., student*
Benefits:	Finding ways for students to demonstrate their strengths in front of their peers • ensures that students with learning differences have opportunities to demonstrate their best thinking publicly; and • can increase students' self-esteem by showing that they have important ideas to share.
Literature:	Wirtz, C. L., Gardner III, R., Weber, K., & Bullara, D. (1996). Using self-correction to improve the spelling performance of low-achieving third graders. *Remedial and Special Education, 17,* 48–58.

Chapter 6:   Establish Positive Classroom Environment

Strategy:	**Create a Nonthreatening Learning Environment**
Focus:	Basic Skills
Area:	Reading; Mathematics/Problem Solving/Calculating; Writing; Social Studies; Science
Learning Difference:	Social Knowledge; Self-Control; Social Behaviors; Self-Confidence
Disability Category:	Serious Emotional Disturbance; Attention Deficit/Hyperactivity Disorder

Tactic Title:	**Solutions for Students Who Are Easily Overwhelmed**
Problem:	Sometimes, students, particularly those with serious emotional disturbance (SED) or ADD/ADHD, are overwhelmed by schoolwork and classroom activities. They may react to this feeling of being overwhelmed by crying in front of peers. Then teasing by peers may ensue, and forming friendships can become even more difficult.
Tactic:	Identify options when students are feeling overwhelmed (e.g., time in a quiet corner of the classroom with a book, movement to a less intense area of the classroom to work with a peer, using a computer to complete the activity). Notify all teachers that a specific object/token is in the student's pocket. If at any point the student feels overwhelmed, the student takes the red plastic triangle, for example, out and puts it in view of the teacher. That red plastic triangle is a cue to the teacher that the work being done or the situation at hand is overwhelming for the student. The student then exercises the prearranged option. The use of unobtrusive nonverbal cues, such as a finger on ear, is also effective.
Example:	Sometimes when I am really really trying to do what I am supposed to, I just can't. I used to just get mad and then I would do dumb things like throw my pencil, push Jacob, make faces or swear . . . everything that would get me in big trouble. Now, my teacher and I have this plan. When I feel like I just can't do something, I put my pencil in a certain position on my desk; this lets my teacher know that I need some time. So, I go to the Library Corner or the Learning Center for a while. It's ok. My teacher and I always talk about what's happening and then we figure out a way for me to go back and try again. Works for me and I think my teacher likes it too.
	Wanda O., student
Benefits:	Using unobtrusive signals • enables teachers to monitor students constantly with simple visual sweeps of the classroom; • enables students to remain active members of the class and make personal choices as to the best learning circumstances for them; • allows students to maintain dignity in front of their peers;

- creates a safe, nonthreatening learning environment for students; and
- lets learning continue for everyone.

Literature: Gunter, P. L., Denny, R. K., Jack, S. L., Shores, R. E., & Nelson, C. M. (1993). Aversive stimuli in academic interactions between students with serious emotional disturbance and their teachers. *Behavioral Disorders, 18,* 265.

PART III

Delivering Instruction

Teaching is systematic presentation of content. Effective teachers present information in carefully monitored lessons that they adjust to meet the needs of their students. In this part of our resource, we describe evidence-based strategies for each principle of delivering instruction.

Component	Principle	Strategy
Delivering Instruction (Part III)	Present Information (Chapter 7)	Gain and Maintain Attention
		Review Prior Skills or Lessons
		Provide Organized, Relevant Lessons
		Show Enthusiasm and Interest
		Use Rewards Effectively
		Consider Level and Student Interest
		Model Thinking Skills
		Teach Fact-Finding Skills
		Teach Divergent Thinking
		Teach Learning Strategies
		Develop Automaticity
		Vary Opportunities for Practice
		Vary Methods of Practice
		Monitor Amount of Work Assigned

(Continued)

(Continued)

Component	Principle	Strategy
	Monitor Presentations (Chapter 8)	Give Immediate, Frequent, Explicit Feedback
		Provide Specific Praise and Encouragement
		Model Correct Performance
		Provide Prompts and Cues
		Check Student Understanding
		Monitor Performance Regularly
		Monitor Performance During Practice
		Use Peers to Improve Instruction
		Provide Opportunities for Success
		Limit Opportunities for Failure
		Monitor Engagement Rates
	Adjust Presentations (Chapter 9)	Adapt Lessons to Meet Student Needs
		Provide Varied Instructional Options
		Alter Pace

Delivering Instruction Works: A Case Study

When young learners are struggling with fine motor control and trying to form numerals and letters correctly, I have found color cues to be very effective. In my classroom, green means "go," yellow means "proceed carefully," and red means "stop." I've created templates for each letter and number with green "start dots," directional arrows, and red "stop dots," so students know where to start a letter/numeral, where to move their pencils, and when to stop. My templates gradually fade out the letters from solid lines to dashes or dots and, finally, just a model at the top of the page and a series of start and stop dots.

I use transparencies with erasable markers so that students can reuse the templates. The templates are stored where students can easily access them to practice whenever they have completed other assignments. They think it's fun to use the markers, and I love the fact that they are totally engaged in learning. (Related tactic is located in Chapter 8: Monitor Presentations under the Strategy: Provide Prompts and Cues.)

Present Information

Component	Principle	Strategy
Delivering Instruction	Present Information	Gain and Maintain Attention
		Review Prior Skills or Lessons
		Provide Organized, Relevant Lessons
		Show Enthusiasm and Interest
		Use Rewards Effectively
		Consider Level and Student Interest
		Model Thinking Skills
		Teach Fact-Finding Skills
		Teach Divergent Thinking
		Teach Learning Strategies
		Develop Automaticity
		Vary Opportunities for Practice
		Vary Methods of Practice
		Monitor Amount of Work Assigned

Chapter 7:   Present Information

Strategy:	**Gain and Maintain Attention**
Focus:	Basic Skills
Area:	Reading; Mathematics/Problem Solving/Calculating
Learning Difference:	Attention; Self-Control; Study Skills
Disability Category:	Attention Deficit/Hyperactivity Disorder
Tactic Title:	**Teacher Proximity**
Problem:	Frequently, students with ADHD have trouble remaining on-task.
Tactic:	Seat the student in an area with few distractions. For example, seat the student away from windows and away from other students who may be distracting. While teaching a lesson, the teacher can stand next to or walk by the student frequently.
Example:	Sometimes, when I am introducing an activity, I'll just walk in Annabelle's direction; it's amazing how quickly she starts paying attention. I also move around the classroom when students are working independently or in small groups so that I can monitor what they are doing. . . . [It] gives me a chance to make notes that I can add to their folders at the end of the day.

Samantha W., teacher

Benefits:	Strategic seating and effective use of teacher proximity

- enable ongoing monitoring of student attention and participation;
- are effective and easy methods of managing disruptive or distracted students;
- are useful tools for recognizing and rewarding appropriate learning behavior;
- can be used with students with any type of learning disability or learning difference; and
- encourage students to be on their best behavior and focus on learning.

Literature:	Bonus, M., & Riordan, L. (1998). *Increasing student on-task behavior through the use of specific seating arrangements* (Master's Action Research Project). Chicago: Saint Xavier University. (ERIC Document Reproduction Service No. ED422129)

Chapter 7: Present Information

Strategy:	**Review Prior Skills or Lessons**
Focus:	Basic Skills
Area:	Reading; Mathematics/Problem Solving/Calculating; Writing; Social Studies; Science; Arts; Fitness
Learning Difference:	Cognition High; Cognition Low; Cognition Mixed; Attention; Memory Short-Term; Memory Long-Term; Receptive Language/Decoding (listening, reading); Expressive Language/Encoding (speaking, writing, spelling); Study Skills
Disability Category:	Specific Learning Disabilities

Tactic Title:	**Linking Instruction and Assessment to Prior Learning**
Problem:	Many students have difficulty seeing the connection between information they have learned previously and current learning and activities. They need a link.
Tactic:	Divide the lesson into three parts:

1. Anticipatory Set:

   First determine skills and content of lessons. Then think about how the new material relates to information covered previously and how it all connects to the real world. Briefly review previously presented ideas/content with examples.

2. During Instruction:

   Give students several opportunities to contribute to the review. Then think of ways to teach and test for competency that will both offer choice and accommodate multiple learning styles. Provide opportunities for open-ended responses that allow students to demonstrate, in their own words, what they have learned. Structure activities that give students opportunities to participate in ways that accommodate their learning styles while allowing them to reject those that do not.

3. Lesson Closure:

   Review lesson objectives, activities, and learning. Remind students why this lesson was important—how their learning will help them in the future. Provide an advanced organizer that tells student how this lesson will be connected to future lessons.

Example:	Here's my basic teaching process:

1. Link today's instruction to previous learning:

   "Yesterday, we learned that /ch/ has several spellings. Knowing this will really help us because today . . .

2. Tell students how that links to today's instruction:

   "Today, we are going to use words with the /ch/ sound to write a story about a good witch."

3. Teach the lesson.

4. Review the lesson:

   "Today, we . . ."

5. Link to tomorrow's learning:

   "Tomorrow, we'll act out our story for Ms. Arnold's class."

If I leave out any of the steps, especially #1, I jeopardize my students' learning.

Greg L., teacher

Benefits: Reviewing prior instruction enables

- teachers to check for student understanding prior to continuing with new material;
- students to review and demonstrate what they know; and
- students to have a structure for their learning.

Literature: Geocaris, C., & Ross, M. (1999). A test worth taking. *Educational Leadership, 57*(1), 29–33.

Chapter 7: Present Information

Strategy:	**Provide Organized, Relevant Lessons**
Focus:	Basic Skills
Area:	Reading, Social Studies; Science
Learning Difference:	Cognition Mixed; Memory Short-Term; Receptive Language/Decoding (listening, reading); Expressive Language/Encoding (speaking, writing, spelling); Processing Verbal Information; Processing Visual Information
Disability Category:	Specific Learning Disabilities; Speech or Language Impairments; Second Language Learning Needs; Serious Emotional Disturbance; Traumatic Brain Injury; Mental Retardation; Attention Deficit/Hyperactivity Disorder; Autism

Tactic Title:	**Concrete Instruction**
Problem:	Teachers find that students with disabilities often have difficulty understanding the difference between "main idea" and "details."
Tactic:	First discuss the concepts of "main idea" and "details" and their relationship to one another. Next give an example. For instance, choose the classroom as the main idea and ask the students to pick details (e.g., chairs, posters, desks) of the classroom. Then have the students fill out a graphic organizer (see Story Map, Part 1) with the main idea as themselves and each of the five smaller attached bubbles with details about themselves. Review the graphic organizer with them by having some students share details and other students decide if the details are correct. Distribute Part 2 of the activity. Read the directions aloud while students follow along. Finally, conclude the activity by recapping the concepts of "main idea" and "details."
Example:	My family came to the United States from Kenya two years ago and I'm still trying very hard to learn English and the American ways. Ms. Devlin is my teacher and I like her very much because she uses "real" things to teach us; sometimes, I don't understand the examples or stories in the books. Today, I learns about "main ideas" and "details." So, I am going to write a story on the computer about "My Family." Ms. Devlin is also very funny and she doesn't draw pictures very well. She makes it easy for me to learn and feel good in school. *Naomi S., student*
Benefits:	Using real-world examples with graphic organizers • provides the extra support/scaffolding that some students require; • models good thinking skills for all students;

- helps students visualize the material; and
- provides a tool that can be applied to other learning activities.

Literature: Marzano, R. J., Pickering, D. J., & Pollack, J. E. (2003). *Classroom instruction that works: Research-based strategies for increasing student achievement.* Alexandria, VA: Association for Supervision and Curriculum Development.

Zadnik, D. (1992). *Instructional supervision in special education: Integrating teacher effectiveness research into model supervisory practices.* Bloomington: Indiana University, School of Education and Council of Administrators of Special Education. (ERIC Document Reproduction Service No. ED358646)

Name _____ Date_____

My Classroom

Story Map
(Part 1)

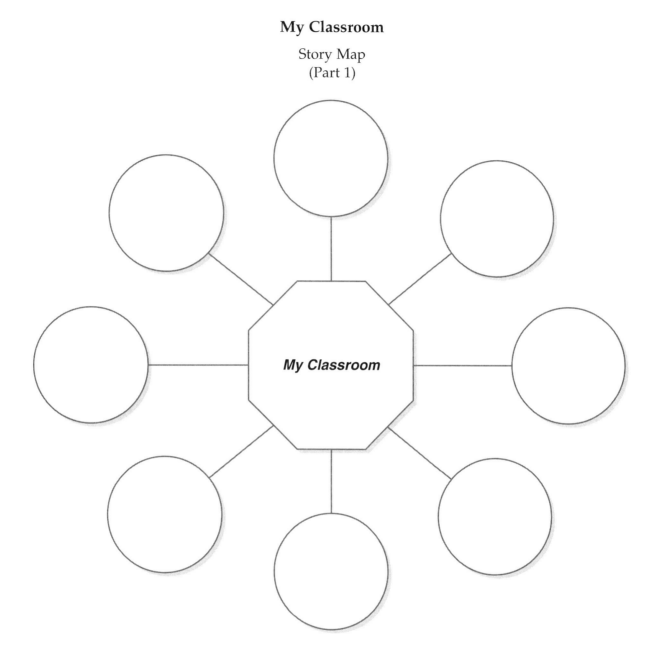

Name _____   Date_____

My Classroom

Story Map
(Part 2)

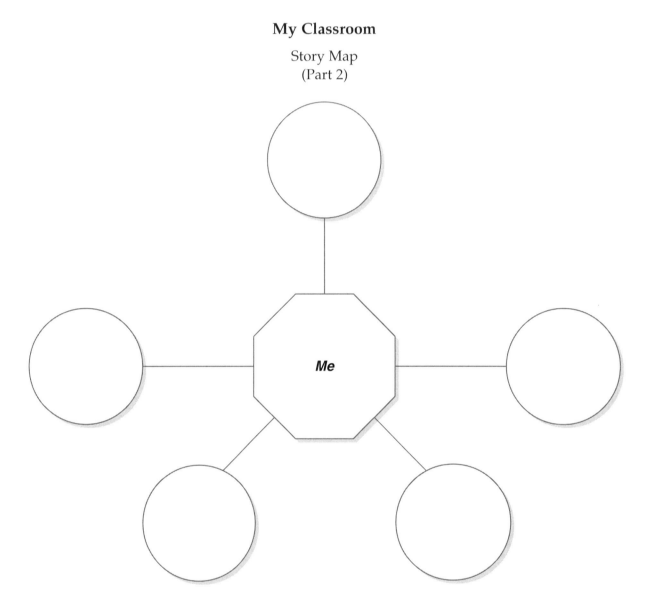

Chapter 7:   Present Information

Strategy:	**Show Enthusiasm and Interest**
Focus:	Basic Skills
Area:	Reading; Mathematics/Problem Solving/Calculating; Writing; Social Studies; Science; Arts; Fitness
Learning Difference:	Self-Confidence
Disability Category:	Mental Retardation; Specific Learning Disabilities; Multiple Disabilities; Attention Deficit/Hyperactivity Disorder; Visual Impairments; Deafness/ Blindness; Gifted and Talented; Traumatic Brain Injury; Hearing Impairments; Second Language Learning Needs; Serious Emotional Disturbance; Speech or Language Impairments; Orthopedic Impairment; Other Health Impairments; Autism

Tactic Title:	**Opportunities to Share**
Problem:	Many students who are not developing at the same academic level as their peers are aware of this discrepancy and consequently display low self-confidence.
Tactic:	Take every opportunity to give all students positive and supportive feedback on their accomplishments. Hold private conferences with students to highlight their individual strengths. Encourage them to share their work. Allow frequent opportunities for students to present and share their drawings, stories, and problem solutions with everyone. Post their work. Highlight their work in newsletters, on your school's Web site, and in personal communication with parents and caregivers.
Example:	I'm always looking for ways to celebrate my students' accomplishments. They need to know that I love it when they learn, so I do silly things sometimes. . . . When they do something wonderful, I "kiss my brain" (fingers to lips and then head), jump up and down (carefully), hug myself, send an e-mail to their parents. We cheer as a class.
	Then they need to please themselves, not just the teacher or others. So I teach them to do the same for themselves.
	Claire T., teacher
Benefits:	When teachers show enthusiasm and interest and provide opportunities for students to share their learning,

- students realize that their work has value;
- students will begin volunteering to share;

- classmates will develop a true appreciation and respect for the accomplishments of others; and
- social interactions among students can improve.

Literature: Epstein, T., & Elias, M. (1996). To reach for the stars: How social/affective education can foster truly inclusive environments. *Phi Delta Kappan, 78,* 157–163.

Chapter 7:   Present Information

Strategy:	**Use Rewards Effectively**

Focus: Basic Skills

Area: Reading; Mathematics/Problem Solving/Calculating; Writing; Social Studies; Science

Learning Difference: Attention; Memory Short-Term; Speaking/Talking; Study Skills; Receptive Language/Decoding (listening, reading); Expressive Language/Encoding (speaking, writing, spelling); Self-Control; Social Behaviors; Self-Confidence

Disability Category: Mental Retardation; Specific Learning Disabilities; Multiple Disabilities; Attention Deficit/Hyperactivity Disorder; Gifted and Talented; Traumatic Brain Injury; Second Language Learning Needs; Serious Emotional Disturbance; Orthopedic or Other Health Impairments; Autism

Tactic Title:	**Taking Charge: Giving Students More Responsibility**

Problem: Teachers often find it difficult to monitor the learning of all students in their class.

Tactic: Use a chart program to show individual student progress. Determine appropriate rewards that are grounded in opportunities for additional learning: computer time, peer time, personal reading time, and/or a learning game.

Tape a chart to each student's desk with the dates for the period and the desired behaviors (paying attention, asking questions, doing homework). Next teach the students how to evaluate themselves at the end of each lesson/day (see Self-Assessment worksheet below). Finally, ask the students how they rated themselves (they can give reasons why).

In the initial phase of the program, reward students based on their evaluations while encouraging honest evaluations. (At least they are paying attention to their behavior, even if their evaluations are not in agreement with those of the teacher). Later, incorporate the teacher's evaluation into the program and give points for "agreements."

Example: I coteach with Ms. Mathis in her fourth-grade classroom. We use learning charts with several students, not just those on my caseload. They really help me monitor student learning/behavior when I'm not in the classroom; also, they help the Planning and Placement Team in making decisions about services for students. Most of all, they enable our students to know exactly where they are in terms of their learning. We've made every effort to ensure that their parents have this information as well. As a special educator, I recommend this tactic to everyone.

Mario L., teacher

Benefits: Using reward systems effectively
- allows students to know what is expected of them;
- teaches students how to monitor their learning all of the time;
- empowers students to take responsibility for their learning;
- promotes appropriate behavior and fosters learning; and
- creates opportunities for conversations about learning among teachers and students.

Literature: Prater, M. A. (1992). Increasing time-on-task in the classroom. *Intervention in School and Clinic, 28*(1), 22–27.

Self-Assessment

Name _____   Date_____

Target Behavior: _____

Rating Scale: 1 = excellent   2 = good   3 = poor

Date/Time	Rating	Evidence
	Total:	

Chapter 7:   Present Information

Strategy:	**Consider Level and Student Interest**

Focus: Basic Skills

Area: Reading; Writing

Learning Difference: Cognition High; Processing Visual Information; Receptive Language/ Decoding (listening, reading); Expressive Language/Encoding (speaking, writing, spelling)

Disability Category: Gifted and Talented

Tactic Title:	**Challenging Students With High Reading and Writing Ability**

Problem: Frequently, students with high reading and writing abilities find reading and writing work at grade level boring and unfulfilling.

Tactic: First identify the high-level readers in your classroom. These students will be your highest-level reading group. Next provide them with reading materials that challenge their ability. For example, give a first grader a book that is divided into chapters. During the reading of the book, provide the student(s) with open-ended questions that require higher-order thinking skills. To challenge writing skills, ask students with varied abilities higher- and lower-level questions that match their ability levels; they must answer their questions in complete sentences. This also enables all learners to use their thinking skills and teach highly skilled learners the art of writing at an advanced level.

Example: I've always found it interesting that "inclusion" just seems to include students with designated disabilities. Well, I believe that every student in my class should have an IEP, so I am always looking for ways to involve all my students. Gifts and Talents isn't a category of disability in our state, so I never assume that they wouldn't benefit from individualized planning and instruction on my part. I seek ways to enrich their learning experiences, to give them opportunities use their talents with other students, and to challenge them constantly to use higher order thinking skills and share their special gifts with everyone.

Javier E., teacher

Benefits: Using open-ended questions
- can stimulate the minds of all levels of readers;
- gives all students, regardless of ability, the opportunity to think critically about a story; and
- can foster students' interests in reading and writing skills that will be very important throughout their lives.

Literature: McGrail, L. (1998). Modifying regular classroom curricula for high ability students. *Gifted Child Today, 21*(2), 36–39.

Chapter 7:   Present Information

Strategy:	**Model Thinking Skills**
Focus:	Basic Skills
Area:	Reading; Mathematics/Problem Solving/Calculating; Writing; Social Studies; Science
Learning Difference:	Receptive Language/Decoding (listening, reading); Expressive Language/ Encoding (speaking, writing, spelling); Processing Visual Information
Disability Category:	Specific Learning Disabilities; Attention Deficit/Hyperactivity Disorder; Traumatic Brain Injury; Second Language Learning Needs; Serious Emotional Disturbance; Speech or Language Impairments; Autism
Tactic Title:	**Teaching Reading and Writing to Students With Reading/Writing Disabilities**
Problem:	Some students who are competent verbally have considerable difficulty reading any assignment, from storybooks to math problems. In addition, although they may draw very well, they may not be able to write.
Tactic:	During silent work time in the general education classroom, provide one-on-one instruction to enable these students to complete picture-oriented worksheets. The content of these worksheets should correspond directly to the topics presented. Model how to write letters and words, and ensure that the student copies the letters and words accurately. Students can keep a journal, dictating beforehand what they want to write, so the teacher can write the student's words and the student can copy or trace the words in the journal. The student then reads aloud what has been written.
Example:	I love using all sorts of variations with journals to enable our students to put their thoughts and feelings on paper, regardless of their abilities/ disabilities. Jodie is my special education coteacher, and together, we've developed appropriate journal "writing" tactics for all of our students. For example,

- Julio uses the computer and dictates his story in Spanish. The computer translates his entry into English; he prints both of his entries. Sometimes, he copies the printouts into his journal. . . . Sometimes he draws a picture, too.

- Matt dictates his entries to Ms. Sylvia, our paraprofessional. She writes down his words; he traces her writing and then draws a picture.
  - Sometimes students work in dyads to record their entries.
  - Some students draw a picture and then dictate the story to a peer or teacher.
  - When students are "stuck," they can select from our Picture Bank.

We're always coming up with new ideas. . . . Bottom line, all students are "writing" in their journals.

Christopher M., teacher

Benefits: When students "write" their own thoughts, they are

- more involved in their learning;
- more likely to remember the words and be able to read them; and
- more likely to carry over the words and letter sounds to subsequent written work.

Literature: Vaughn, S., Hughes, M. T., Schumm, J. S., & Klingner, J. (1998). A collaborative effort to enhance reading and writing instruction in inclusion classrooms. *Learning Disabilities Quarterly, 21,* 57–74.

Chapter 7:   Present Information

Strategy:	**Teach Fact-Finding Skills**
Focus:	Basic Skills
Area:	Reading
Learning Difference:	Study Skills; Receptive Language/Decoding (listening, reading); Expressive Language/Encoding (speaking, writing, spelling)
Disability Category:	Specific Learning Disabilities
Tactic Title:	**Using a Story Grammar Marker to Improve Reading Comprehension**
Problem:	Frequently, students with learning disabilities require additional support to recall all the parts of a story that they have just read.
Tactic:	To improve reading comprehension, use a visual reminder of the different parts of a story, such as a story grammar marker (see Story Shapes). First construct the marker with the student while explaining the significance of the different pieces. Glue felt shapes along the length of an 18" piece of ribbon. The shapes represent the various aspects of a typical elementary-level story, such as the main character, the setting, the problem, the attempts to solve the problem, internal response of the characters, and conclusion. Students can suggest shapes that would be most helpful to them, or teachers can use standard shapes, such as a star for the main character and a heart for the internal response.
Example:	To enhance my students' writing skills, I encourage them to stop at the end of each paragraph (or page, depending on how long the story is) and write down the important story components that were mentioned in that section of the story. They should also write down any other things they thought were important to the story so that they have notes to refer to when they start writing a paper. *Bea B., teacher*
Benefits:	Visual reminders enable students to • review a story they have read; • review their writing; • remember the necessary components in a short story; • stay on track when reading; and • recognize the important components of a story.
Literature:	Johnson, L., Graham, S., & Harris, K. R. (1997). The effects of goal setting and self-instruction on learning a reading comprehension strategy: A study of students with learning disabilities. *Journal of Learning Disabilities, 30,* 80–91.

Name _____   Date _____

Story Shapes

Chapter 7: Present Information

Strategy:	**Teach Divergent Thinking**

Focus: Basic Skills

Area: Reading, Social Studies

Learning Difference: Receptive Language/Decoding (listening, reading); Processing Visual Information

Disability Category: Specific Learning Disabilities; Traumatic Brain Injury; Speech or Language Impairments; Second Language Learning Needs; Serious Emotional Disturbance; Autism

Tactic Title:	**Reading Organizers**

Problem: Students enjoy reading when they understand the meaning of what they read.

Tactic: Make an organizer worksheet for students with headings such as main characters, problem in the story, etc. The headings should represent the parts of the story that students need to comprehend to understand the story as a whole. These headings should indicate what is important, and they should serve as guides while the student is reading. As they read, students record the information from the story on the worksheet under the correct headings. Before students do this by themselves, teachers, paraprofessionals, and other volunteers can model using the organizer for students.

Example: These worksheets are so helpful in teaching students how to "organize" their thinking . . . to know that they need to be looking for certain features in a story and be able to support their choices. I also use a similar organizer for different types of writing assignments. Of course, we make modifications for different learners. . . . Some draw pictures to represent the parts; some dictate to a peer or paraprofessional. There a lots of ways to use this tactic and adapt it to individual student needs.

Maggie H., teacher

Benefits: Using graphic organizers help students to
- remember more about the story by recording information as they read; and
- think as they read, which helps them understand the story in parts and as a whole.

Literature: Swanson, P. (1998). Teaching effective comprehension strategies to students with learning and reading disabilities. *Intervention in School and Clinic, 33,* 209–218.

Chapter 7: Present Information

Strategy:	**Teach Learning Strategies**
Focus:	Basic Skills
Area:	Mathematics/Problem Solving/Calculating
Learning Difference:	Cognition Mixed; Processing Visual Information; Attention; Memory Long-Term; Memory Short-Term
Disability Category:	Specific Learning Disabilities

Tactic Title:	**Encouraging Mental Computation**
Problem:	Sometimes students struggle with mental computation in mathematics.
Tactic:	Many students are not able to compute "in their heads." First allow students to use strategies that are effective for them in computation. These strategies may include counting on their fingers or using a number line or manipulatives (blocks, cubes, etc.). Next remove all supports so that they must use an alternative to solve the problem. Then provide another addition problem and ask them to visualize the blocks or hands in their heads. Finally, continue with additional problems in this way and encourage the use of mental addition.
Example:	Using manipulatives is the starting point for learning simple math calculations. I remember Rebecca; when counting, she literally needed to touch her finger to her forehead as she said each number to be sure she was making one-to-one correspondence. Some of my students need to use manipulatives longer or whenever a new concept is introduced. In fact, I remember when I was taking a course on multiple regression in my master's program, I needed colored acetate circles that let me "see" the process. I've learned that it is important for students to understand the concepts before taking away manipulatives. *Sal R., teacher*
Benefits:	Teaching students strategies such as "computing in their heads" enables them to • visualize their learning; • improve mental computation; and • bridge the use of concrete materials to abstract thinking.
Literature:	Fleischner, J. E., & Manheimer, M. A. (1997). Math interventions for students with learning disabilities: Myths and realities. *School Psychology Review, 26,* 397–413.

Chapter 7:   Present Information

Strategy:	**Develop Automaticity**

Focus: Basic Skills

Area: Writing

Learning Difference: Expressive Language/Encoding (speaking, writing, spelling); Fine Motor (handwriting, articulation, etc.)

Disability Category: Specific Learning Disabilities

Tactic Title:	**Tracing Writing Through Plexiglas**

Problem: Students who are beginning writers may find it difficult to reproduce letters correctly.

Tactic: Obtain a piece of clear Plexiglas. Type or write the student's name (or other writing example) using a large font size. Lightly tape the printout to the back of the Plexiglas. Teach the student to trace the letters with a dry erase marker. Then tell the student to erase the writing. Allow the student to perform the task as many times as desired or give a specific number of times to perform the task. Give the student several opportunities to view the Plexiglas writing separately from the printout, against a blank piece of paper.

Example: I've used this tactic with students learning either manuscript or cursive writing. They can practice individual letters, words, and even sentences . . . a nice integration of fine motor practice with their dictated journal entries. I've also used transparencies that I tape to their desks; the practice sheets that are placed underneath can be adapted for individual students and used repeatedly. For those who need opportunities to practice with larger motor movements, I place the transparency on an overhead projector so that students can trace with chalk or paintbrushes dipped in water or an erasable marker on the whiteboard. I can adjust the size of the letters by the distance of the projector from the board.

Lindsay A., teacher

Benefits: Using transparencies or Plexiglas for fine motor practice
- enables students to become familiar with the hand movements necessary to produce legible writing;
- develops fine motor automaticity; and
- helps students gain confidence in their ability to reproduce letters rapidly and accurately.

Literature: Graham, S., & Harris, K. R. (2006). Preventing writing difficulties: Providing additional handwriting and spelling instruction to at-risk children in first grade. *Teaching Exceptional Children, 38*(5), 64–66.

Chapter 7: Present Information

Strategy:	**Vary Opportunities for Practice**
Focus:	Basic Skills
Area:	Arts
Learning Difference:	Fine Motor (handwriting, articulation, etc.); Gross Motor (running, walking, etc.); Expressive Language/Encoding (speaking, writing, spelling)
Disability Category:	Specific Learning Disabilities; Attention Deficit/Hyperactivity Disorder

Tactic Title:	**Using the Arts to Help Students Learn**
Problem:	Students with learning disabilities frequently have trouble learning in a traditional way. They have difficulty expressing themselves verbally, using fine motor skills, and remaining on-task.
Tactic:	Use the arts (e.g., drawing, storytelling, acting, painting, singing, dancing) to help students learn. For example, in kindergarten, to teach students about what being a friend is, set up different centers in the classroom that teach students about friendship. For the art center, supply students with materials to draw or paint a picture about friendship. At the reading center, read a story about friendship using puppets. Provide students with an opportunity to create their own stories using the puppets and show them to the class. At the acting center, provide costume clothes for children to dress up and act out their friendship stories. At the listening center, provide songs about friendship for students to listen to and assist them in making up their own songs about friendship to familiar tunes (e.g., "Mary Had a Little Lamb," "Twinkle, Twinkle Little Star"). At the dancing center, show students friendship dances.
Example:	I've found that giving students other ways to learn really supports and expands traditional instruction. With my older students, I use learning centers and role-playing activities. I've also found that our art, music, and physical education teachers are really cooperative about integrating classroom learning objectives into their classes. For example, when I told Mr. Henry that we were focusing on similarities and differences, he developed a wonderful series of art lessons to correspond. *Carlos T., teacher*
Benefits:	Using the arts • engages every student by providing a wide variety of learning opportunities involving all of the senses; • enables all students, regardless of ability or disability, to be successful;

- integrates the arts as a method of teaching regular academic subjects;
- expands learning opportunities by using different media; and
- promotes overall intelligence and generalizations of concepts.

Literature: Gallas, K. (1991). Arts as epistemology: Enabling children to know what they know. *Harvard Educational Review, 61,* 93–105.

Chapter 7: Present Information

Strategy:	**Vary Methods of Practice**
Focus:	Basic Skills
Area:	Writing
Learning Difference:	Receptive Language/Decoding (listening, reading); Expressive Language/Encoding (speaking, writing, spelling); Processing Visual Information; Processing Verbal Information; Self-Confidence
Disability Category:	Speech or Language Impairments; Traumatic Brain Injury; Mental Retardation; Second Language Learning Needs; Specific Learning Disabilities; Serious Emotional Disturbance; Attention Deficit/ Hyperactivity Disorder; Autism; Orthopedic Impairments; Other Health Impairments

Tactic Title:	**Using Technology to Enhance Reading and Writing**
Problem:	Creating stories is an excellent way for students to express themselves and improve their writing skills. However, students who struggle with phonics or have physical disabilities may find the writing part of this task difficult and frustrating.
Tactic:	Assistive technology enhances student learning by enabling students to "bypass" the challenges of a particular learning difference or disability. For example, students with fine motor control issues often find that a pencil grip provides more control. Those with less than normal visual acuity benefit from large print on paper and on a computer. Finally, many of these programs can be adjusted to repeat a word, sentence, paragraph, or an entire story. Students type their stories, and as the student types in a word and presses the space bar, the computer repeats the word. If the word repeated is the word the student wants, then the student can continue. Other systems, such as Alpha Smart, allow students to type combination keystrokes, enhance fine motor control, provide large-display font size, and enhance spelling and grammar in writing and communicating. These tools can be used whenever a writing assignment is presented, including writing essays, term papers, taking notes in class, or completing an exam. Once the student has completed the assignment, remind the student to spell-check the assignment. Finally, allow the student to connect the system to a printer to print out the work.
Example:	I remember many, many years ago, when the first computers were brought into our school. My principal thought the best use would be to create a computer lab so that all students would have access. Somehow, I was able to snag an Apple computer and dot matrix printer for my

resource room. I had to write the documentation for the word processing program myself. What a transformation! All of a sudden, my non-writers wanted to write all the time. They would do anything for time on the computer. So I often had them work in pairs . . . writing, editing, and publishing. The best part was, and still is, that all my students can use the technology, and now there are so many new ways to adapt the input and output. I couldn't teach without it.

Emily K., teacher

Example: I love using the computer to write my stories because they don't have to be perfect the first time. I can just write and edit as I go or do it later. I use my headphones to listen to the words. Sometimes I listen as I write and sometimes I wait until I've finished a whole sentence or paragraph. I try to fix all the spelling and grammar myself before using the spell/grammar checkers. I keep track of my trouble words or errors so I can practice them later. The best part is deciding if I want to publish my work for our classroom library.

Sasha C., student

Benefits: Using technology to enhance writing

- enables students with physical disabilities to complete assignments on time, neatly, and with few errors;
- allows students to take notes that they will be able to read later because they can print out a copy, enlarge the font, and make other changes;
- allows both students and teacher to focus on the actual finished product, rather than the process of completing the assignment and the mishaps that may occur along the way;
- enables students to be successful;
- includes students with physical disabilities while maintaining learning and production expectations for all students;
- is an excellent accommodation for other students who are challenged by the writing process;
- helps students who have a story in mind but cannot express their thoughts on paper;
- provides a way for students to draft, edit, publish, and share their writing with others; and
- lets students hear their writing aloud, which helps with comprehension skills.

Literature: AlphaSmart Direct Inc. (2008). *AlphaSmart™*. Retrieved January 6, 2008, from http://www.alphasmart.com

Cohen, M. (1993). Machines for thinking: The computer's role in schools. *Educational and Training Technology International, 30,* 57.

Lewis, R. B. (1998). Assistive technology and learning disabilities: Today's realities and tomorrow's promises. *Journal of Learning Disabilities, 31,* 16–26.

Chapter 7:   Present Information

Strategy:	**Monitor Amount of Work Assigned**
Focus:	Basic Skills
Area:	Reading
Learning Difference:	Receptive Language/Decoding (listening, reading); Expressive Language/Encoding (speaking, writing, spelling); Fine Motor (handwriting, articulation, etc.); Self-Confidence
Disability Category:	Speech or Language Impairments; Second Language Learning Needs; Serious Emotional Disturbance; Specific Learning Disabilities; Attention Deficit/Hyperactivity Disorder; Autism
Tactic Title:	**Using Educational Games to Enhance Student Involvement and Motivation**
Problem:	Both teachers and students can become frustrated when traditional reading methods do not work. Reading/phonics games can be effective instructional tools.
Tactic:	At a minimum of once per week in a 45-minute time block, the teacher and student should have a one-on-one interaction. During this time, play a phonics board game where correctly identifying sounds and words enables players to move forward on the game board. After a player wins, the player reads a "little book" that incorporates the phonics sounds and words used in the game. Record the student reading the book aloud. Finally, listen to the recordings each week and monitor the progress and improvements in the student's reading. These interactions provide data and evidence for the teacher so that appropriate amounts of work can be planned for the future.
Example:	I love my conference time with my teacher. Every week we spend 15 minutes together and no one is allowed to interrupt us. Usually, we play a game and then I read or we look at my writing or something like that. Sometimes she tapes my reading or our conversation. Then she asks me what she can do to make learning better for me! Wow! Then we make a plan for the next week . . . how many spelling words, which books, how many math problems, and so on. She makes me feel very special. *Juan L., student*
Benefits:	One-on-one conferences/interactions • give students the opportunity not only to have fun with learning but also to spend personal time with their teacher;

- provide both students and teachers with the opportunity to monitor learning; and
- let students know that their success is important to the teacher.

Literature: Morgan, M., & Moni, K. B. (2007). Motivate students with disabilities using sight-vocabulary activities. *Intervention in School & Clinic, 48,* 229–233.

Monitor Presentations

Component	Principle	Strategy
Delivering Instruction	Monitor Presentations	Give Immediate, Frequent, Explicit Feedback
		Provide Specific Praise and Encouragement
		Model Correct Performance
		Provide Prompts and Cues
		Check Student Understanding
		Monitor Performance Regularly
		Monitor Performance During Practice
		Use Peers to Improve Instruction
		Provide Opportunities for Success
		Limit Opportunities for Failure
		Monitor Engagement Rates

Chapter 8: Monitor Presentations

Strategy:	**Give Immediate, Frequent, Explicit Feedback**
Focus:	Content Skills
Area:	Fitness
Learning Difference:	Social Knowledge; Self-Control; Social Behaviors; Self-Confidence
Disability Category:	Autism

Tactic Title:	**Teaching the Concept of Win/Lose to Students With Autism Spectrum Disorders**
Problem:	Students with autism often have difficulty understanding the concept of win/lose.
Tactic:	Ensure high rates of success for students. Give explicit verbal praise that tells students exactly why they were successful. Provide praise for all accomplishments, even if the entire goal is not fully met (e.g., "That was a great job. You really wanted to win and played very hard, but I heard you say something unkind when you lost. Next time, I want you to try it this way . . .). Ensure that goals are attainable and make sure that goals are met using small, manageable steps.
Example:	In addition to providing appropriate feedback with my students, I've also used social stories to reinforce the concepts of win and lose. The stories teach students that everyone wins sometimes and everyone loses sometimes. All the students in my PE class benefit from these stories as well. I've also talked with classroom teachers about integrating concepts such as win/lose into their instruction. In this way, students get the message more than once. *Ned T., teacher*
Benefits:	Providing immediate, frequent, explicit feedback • encourages students to keep trying; • provides support for their accomplishments; • gives students the information they need to improve performance/learning; and • makes learning tasks manageable when feedback is given at frequent intervals.
Literature:	Crozier, S., & Tincani, M. J. (2005). Using a modified social story to decrease disruptive behavior of a child with autism. *Focus on Autism and Other Developmental Disabilities, 20,* 150–157. Rhizzo, T., Faison-Hodge, J., Woodard, R., & Sayers, K. (2003). Factors affecting social experiences in inclusive physical education. *Adapted Physical Activity Quarterly, 20*(3), 317.

Chapter 8:   Monitor Presentations

Strategy:	**Provide Specific Praise and Encouragement**

Focus: Basic Skills

Area: Writing

Learning Difference: Cognition Mixed; Fine Motor (handwriting, articulation, etc.); Processing Verbal Information; Expressive Language/Encoding (speaking, writing, spelling)

Disability Category: Specific Learning Disabilities

Tactic Title:	**Interactive Writing**

Problem: Some students have difficulty with sound/symbol relationships, spelling, or the mechanics of writing.

Tactic: Elicit student participation in writing sentences or paragraphs by asking questions to guide students towards the creation of a complete sentence about a specific topic. As the students determine each word of the sentence, request that one student come to the easel and write the word. Then ask other students if they have any comments about what was written. This is when mini-lessons about spelling, the mechanics of writing, and other topics can be addressed. Always correct student mistakes in a positive manner. Ask other students for suggestions as to how to make the word better or indicate to the writer that something needs to be fixed rather than saying it is wrong.

Example: Students learn so much through modeling from both their peers and their teacher, especially when they are providing support and new ideas. I've found this method is especially effective with those students who may be reluctant to write independently. I am also able to monitor my students' learning and make notes as to future topics for mini-lessons or individual instruction.

Paul T., teacher

Benefits: Using this tactic
- involves the entire class in writing.
- teaches students the mechanics of writing, as well as word choices.
- increases the students' confidence in writing.

Literature: Armstrong, D. C. (1994). Gifted child's education requires real dialogue: The use of interactive writing for collaborative education. *Gifted Child Quarterly, 38,* 136–145.

Chapter 8: Monitor Presentations

Strategy:	**Model Correct Performance**
Focus:	Basic Skills
Area:	Reading
Learning Difference:	Expressive Language/Encoding (speaking, writing, spelling)
Disability Category:	Mental Retardation; Specific Learning Disabilities; Attention Deficit/ Hyperactivity Disorder; Traumatic Brain Injury; Second Language Learning Needs; Speech or Language Impairments; Autism

Tactic Title:	**Spell and Say**
Problem:	Students become frustrated when they have difficulty spelling words and forming sentences. Students often do not associate the correct sound with the correct letter, causing them to print the wrong letter on the page.
Tactic:	Sound each word phoneme by phoneme while at the same time writing the word on paper or on the board slowly. Then tell the students to print the word independently. Check for proper spelling and form. When the students have finished, ask them to sound out the word slowly. Continue proceeding until the entire sentence is written. Check for grammar.
Example:	When I use this tactic with the whole class, my special education coteacher or my paraprofessional circulate in the room and monitor student performance. At other times, we use this tactic in small groups or with individual students. It's also appropriate for peer tutoring sessions.

Kendra S., teacher

Benefits:	When teachers model correct spelling and writing mechanics, students

- begin to recognize the sound-letter connection along with sentence structure and style;
- are not practicing errors; and
- learn to write independently.

Literature:	Clarke-Klein, S. M. (1994). Expressive phonological deficiencies: Impact on spelling development. *Topics in Language Disorders, 14,* 40.

Chapter 8:   Monitor Presentations

Strategy:	**Provide Prompts and Cues**
Focus:	Basic Skills
Area:	Reading
Learning Difference:	Attention; Speaking/Talking; Self-Control; Processing Visual Information; Receptive Language/Decoding (listening, reading); Expressive Language/Encoding (speaking, writing, spelling)
Disability Category:	Speech or Language Impairments; Second Language Learning Needs; Specific Learning Disabilities

Tactic Title:	**Red Light, Green Light**
Problem:	Frequently, students with reading disabilities read paragraphs as one whole sentence rather than pausing at commas and stopping at periods.
Tactic:	First take one paragraph and highlight the beginning word of each sentence in green. Then highlight every comma in yellow and every period in red. To introduce the use of punctuation and how to inflect your voice while reading, begin the lesson with a discussion of traffic lights and what the colors green, yellow, and red represent. Then give each student a copy of the paragraph that has been highlighted. Tell the students that a green word signifies the beginning of a sentence where they should begin to read. When the students see a yellow comma, they should slow down and pause. At every red period, the students should stop, take a breath, and then continue reading. After students become familiar with this tactic, begin to increase the number of paragraphs.
Example:	I've used this tactic in my music classes. For example, green could symbolize the beginning of a musical phrase, yellow could symbolize a breath mark in the middle of the phrase, and red might symbolize a fermata or the ending of a phrase where a note is being held. It works equally as well for choral and instrumental pieces. *Anthony A., teacher*
Benefits:	Using color coding • is a useful instructional technique for all students, especially those with reading disabilities; • can teach students how to decipher punctuation marks and also how to use inflection in their voices while reading orally and speaking; and • can be applied to letter and numeral formation.
Literature:	Eakin, S., & Douglas, V. (1971). Automatization and oral reading problems in children. *Journal of Learning Disabilities, 4,* 31–38. Goolsby, T. W. (1999). Assessment in instrumental music. *Music Educators Journal, 95,* 31.

Chapter 8: Monitor Presentations

Strategy:	**Check Student Understanding**
Focus:	Basic Skills
Area:	Reading
Learning Difference:	Processing Visual Information; Receptive Language/Decoding (listening, reading); Self-Confidence
Disability Category:	Specific Learning Disabilities; Attention Deficit/Hyperactivity Disorder
Tactic Title:	**Retrospective Miscue Analysis (RMA)**
Problem:	Many students have difficulty reading (decoding and comprehension).
Tactic:	First audiotape the student reading and retelling a story. The reader then listens to the tape while following along in the original text and discusses selected miscues with the teacher (e.g., why it was made, if it made sense, how much it resembled the printed text, if it was corrected, or if it needed to be corrected). Over time, readers develop and use strategies for constructing the meaning of a text.
Example:	The RMA tactic aids students in understanding that reading is not only about recognizing words but also about constructing meaning. Students no longer use "sounding out the word" or "asking the teacher" as ways of figuring out a word. Instead, they are more likely to skip over the word, go back, and see what word makes sense in the context of the sentence. They are taking responsibility for their own learning. *John L., teacher*
Benefits:	Retrospective miscue analysis (RMA) • improves student self-confidence; • gives students a strategy to improve their reading; • can be adapted to other content areas; and • can be used by peers and professionals as well.
Literature:	Martens, P. (1998). Using retrospective miscue analysis to inquire: Learning from Michael. *The Reading Teacher, 52,* 176–180.

Chapter 8:   Monitor Presentations

Strategy:	**Monitor Performance Regularly**
Focus:	Basic Skills
Area:	Reading; Mathematics/Problem Solving/Calculating; Writing; Social Studies; Science
Learning Difference:	Attention; Study Skills; Social Knowledge; Self-Control; Receptive Language/Decoding (listening, reading); Self-Confidence; Expressive Language/Encoding (speaking, writing, spelling); Processing Verbal Information
Disability Category:	Autism; Second Language Learning Needs; Serious Emotional Disturbance; Attention Deficit/Hyperactivity Disorder

Tactic Title:	**Using a Schedule to Reduce Anxiety and Increase Achievement**
Problem:	Many students are unable to remain focused and accomplish their assignments when they feel uncomfortable with the tasks and with their surroundings.
Tactic:	Design a simple daily schedule format that includes blank spaces for each specific subject area reflecting a day's activities. Do not make a schedule that reflects the whole week's activities, because it may raise students' anxiety levels. Leave a column of at least one inch where you can reinforce students with comments, happy faces, stickers, or simply provide additional feedback. Break down the activities within each subject area so that students can follow along easily and check each task when completed. After the completion of all activities within one subject area, check the student's work, provide necessary feedback, and place a sticker or any other type of reinforcement under the appropriate column. As the student's behavior and academic skills reflect some improvement, continue to reinforce them intermittently. At the end of each day, discuss any issues regarding the student's work reflected on the schedule and sign the schedule along with the student.
Example:	I've used various forms of charts to monitor student performance throughout the day. They not only help the student (and me) keep on top of things, my paraprofessional and special education teacher have said that the charts enable them to "jump right in" because they can see what is expected and what has been accomplished. I also send the charts home each day for parents to review, sign, and return to me the next morning. That way, we are in constant communication about their children and can be consistent in our expectations.

Sandra P., teacher

Benefits: Using schedules to monitor student performance
- provides clear guidelines for learning and behavior expectations;
- can reduce student anxiety;
- provides ongoing information regarding student performance; and
- informs and provides students with easy guidelines that will help them accomplish their schoolwork and reduce their anxiety levels.

Literature: Dollard, N., & Christensen, L. (1996). Constructive classroom management. *Focus on Exceptional Children, 29,* 1–11.

Chapter 8:   Monitor Presentations

Strategy:	**Monitor Performance During Practice**
Focus:	Basic Skills
Area:	Reading; Mathematics/Problem Solving/Calculating; Writing; Social Studies; Science
Learning Difference:	Attention; Receptive Language/Decoding (listening, reading); Expressive Language/Encoding (speaking, writing, spelling); Processing Verbal Information; Processing Visual Information; Self-Control; Self-Confidence
Disability Category:	Attention Deficit/Hyperactivity Disorder

Tactic Title:	**One-on-One Work With Students**
Problem:	Many students have difficulty remaining involved in classroom activities.
Tactic:	If possible, work with students as much as possible on a one-on-one basis. If this is not possible, increase physical proximity to students while they are working in groups. Your proximity will increase their attention. In addition, work pauses into your routine. After several minutes of focused academic work, let students take a short break, preferably with work more desirable to the student but occasionally just to relax.
Example:	I find that working more closely with students allows for more accurate monitoring of their attention and their work. Also, I can provide more immediate feedback, especially positive feedback, more frequently, which also helps them remain on-task. *Sherrill S., teacher*
Benefits:	Finding opportunities to work more frequently with students individually • enables teachers to monitor student performance more accurately; • increases students' time on-task and their self-confidence; and • tells students that their teachers value them as learners.
Literature:	Gardill, M. C., DuPaul, G. J., & Kyle, K. E. (1996). Classroom strategies for managing students with attention-deficit/hyperactivity disorder. *Intervention in School and Clinic, 32,* 89–94.

Chapter 8:   Monitor Presentations

Strategy:	**Use Peers to Improve Instruction**
Focus:	Basic Skills
Area:	Reading; Mathematics/Problem Solving/Calculating; Social Studies; Science
Learning Difference:	Attention; Processing Visual Information; Self-Control; Expressive Language/Encoding (speaking, writing, spelling); Processing Verbal Information
Disability Category:	Attention Deficit/Hyperactivity Disorder

Tactic Title:	**Peer Tutoring in the General Education Classroom**
Problem:	Some students have difficulty remaining attentive and involved in whole-group instruction.
Tactic:	Introduce a new topic to the class (for example, a new vocabulary list). Depending on the content of the lesson, pair students either randomly or based on ability. Appoint a "tutor" and a "tutee" in each pair. Provide the tutor with an answer sheet for the lesson (e.g., correct spelling and pronunciation guides). For the first ten minutes, the tutor previews vocabulary and elicits responses from the tutee. Then students review spelling, pronunciation, and definitions and practice using the vocabulary words in sentences. After ten minutes, students swap roles; the tutor becomes the tutee and is taught by the new tutor.
Example:	I've used peer tutoring for several years in all kinds of learning activities. Students recognize that we can all learn from one another, and they develop a sense of responsibility for one another. I teach the tutors how to tutor and monitor their tutoring sessions. Everyone gets to be a tutor and a tutee at some point. I believe that peer tutoring has been a wonderful way to build a community of learners in my classroom.

Alicia T., teacher

Benefits:	Peer tutoring

- allows all students to interact with their peers and remain focused while actively engaging in a learning activity;
- can boost students' self-esteem; and
- is a great way to match students with similar learning disabilities and ability levels.

Literature:	Arreaga-Mayer, C. (1998). Increasing active student responding and improving academic performance through classwide peer tutoring. *Intervention in School and Clinic, 34,* 89–94.

Chapter 8:   Monitor Presentations

Strategy:	**Provide Opportunities for Success**

Focus: Basic Skills

Area: Reading; Mathematics/Problem Solving/Calculating; Writing; Social Studies; Science

Learning Difference: Attention; Processing Visual Information; Cognition Mixed; Cognition High; Cognition Low; Hearing; Memory Short-Term; Memory Long-Term; Speaking/Talking; Study Skills; Fine Motor (handwriting, articulation, etc.); Gross Motor (running, walking, etc.); Processing Verbal Information; Receptive Language/Decoding (listening, reading)

Disability Category: Attention Deficit/Hyperactivity Disorder; Deafness/Blindness; Hearing Impairments; Mental Retardation; Multiple Disabilities; Traumatic Brain Injury; Second Language Learning Needs; Serious Emotional Disturbance; Specific Learning Disabilities; Speech or Language Impairments; Orthopedic Impairments; Other Health Impairments; Autism

Tactic Title:	**Using Visual Aids to Help Students Learn**

Problem: Teachers are often unfamiliar with ways to incorporate visual aids to hold students' attention and to help those struggling with certain lessons.

Tactic: When introducing new material, it is often helpful to provide visual aids (manipulatives, charts, graphs). For example, when describing the parts of flowers and their importance in the fertilization process, students can select real plants. First give the students specific guidelines on what to look for, possibly in the form of handouts with examples and with plant parts labeled. Next allow the students to find their own unique examples within the guidelines. Give them an allotted time frame to do so. Have each student present that student's selected example to the class.

Example: I rely on all sorts of visual aids when teaching word recognition. For example, to help students "see" the differences in the size and shape of individual letters, "tall letters" such as *f, l,* and *h* are blue; "small letters" such as *a, e,* and *n* are red; and "tail letters" such as *g* and *y* are green. I use the code when I write words on the board or the easel and also on student worksheets. I use transparencies with the worksheets so that I can reuse the color-coded worksheets. I also have the color-coded letters cut into 1 × 2 inch pieces so that we can build words. Sometimes seeing the overall shape of the word in color helps students remember it. This tactic works especially well with sight words.

Cathy J., teacher

Benefits: Visual aids

           • can enable students to become actively involved in the learning process;
           • help students who struggle with focusing on the lesson by providing a focal point for their attention; and
           • support learning for many students, not just those with disabilities.

Literature: Friar, K. K. (1999). Changing voices, changing times. *Music Educators Journal, 86,* 26–29.

Chapter 8:   Monitor Presentations

Strategy:	**Limit Opportunities for Failure**
Focus:	Basic Skills
Area:	Arts
Learning Difference:	Cognition Low; Fine Motor (handwriting, articulation, etc.)
Disability Category:	Mental Retardation; Specific Learning Disabilities; Traumatic Brain Injury; Orthopedic Impairments; Other Health Impairments; Autism

Tactic Title:	**Accommodating Differences in the Music Classroom**
Problem:	Diverse learners require teachers to develop creative accommodations to address the learning needs of all students.
Tactic:	Elementary music curricula typically include teaching students about the recorder and how to play it. Some students with disabilities may find that the music class is one of the few classes throughout the day where they can participate with other classmates; therefore, it is very important for them to be included as much as possible. Provide extra assistance for students with cognitive and/or fine motor deficits, because they may have difficulty moving their fingers from note to note with the same dexterity as their classmates. Consider limiting the number of notes that individual students need to remember and play. In some cases, a single note may be adequate.
Example:	I use all sorts of tactics to accommodate students who have difficulty with fine motor tasks, such as writing. They use bigger pencils, pencils/pens with rubber grippers, paper with larger spaces between the lines, or paper with raised or color-coded lines. I modify writing paper by coloring in the space where the small letters (*a, e, i,* etc.) are placed. We call it "rainbow writing" because I change the colors on different days. I use square crayons, so it really doesn't take long at all. *Alec P., teacher*
Benefits:	Accommodating individual differences • includes all students, including those with limited abilities; • gives students a sense of accomplishment; • lets students know that they "belong"; and • can be used with many fine motor tasks, such as writing, typing, or buttoning.
Literature:	de l'Etoile, S. (1996). Meeting the needs of the special learner in music. *American Music Teacher, 45,* 10–13.

Chapter 8: Monitor Presentations

Strategy:	**Monitor Engagement Rates**
Focus:	Basic Skills
Area:	Fitness
Learning Difference:	Attention; Memory Short-Term; Self-Control; Social Behaviors; Self-Confidence
Disability Category:	Attention Deficit/Hyperactivity Disorder

Tactic Title:	**Using Exercise for Students With Attention Deficit Disorder**
Problem:	Physicians and educators frequently recommend medication as the only treatment for students with attention deficit/hyperactivity disorder.
Tactic:	There are alternatives to medication. For example, first allow students to discuss their favorite type of exercise and/or activity. Then students and teachers come to an agreement on which activity the group will engage in collectively two to three times a week. Record students' attention span in the classroom and monitor progress of each student. Also note whether the activity is decreasing the students' stress levels, which is the main goal of the activity. Finally, once a week, students and teachers discuss the progress of the activity and its effect on controlling stress levels. Focus on the importance of relieving stress through exercise, which helps with focusing attention.
Example:	Several of my students really need to "let off some steam" now and then. It's been so helpful to work with Mr. Sorensen, our physical education teacher. Together with my students, we've come up with some simple exercises that we can do in the classroom at least once a day. Gets me moving, too. I also let my students move around the classroom or stand up when they are working, as long as they don't interfere with the learning of other students. So far, our data show substantial improvement in student attention.

Arlene B., teacher

Benefits:	Using physical activity

- is a great way to help students deal with the stress they might feel in the classroom;
- allows students and teacher to make changes if the program is not working;
- can decrease the reliance on medication for students with attention deficit/hyperactivity disorder; and
- encourages students to engage in a healthy alternative to medication.

Literature:	Higdon, H. (1999). Getting their attention. *Runner's World, 34,* 84.

9

Adjust Presentations

Component	Principle	Strategy
Delivering Instruction	Adjust Presentations	Adapt Lessons to Meet Student Needs
		Provide Varied Instructional Options
		Alter Pace

Chapter 9: Adjust Presentations

Strategy:	**Adapt Lessons to Meet Student Needs**
Focus:	Basic Skills
Area:	Reading; Mathematics/Problem Solving/Calculating; Writing; Social Studies; Science
Learning Difference:	Attention; Study Skills; Receptive Language/Decoding (listening, reading); Fine Motor (handwriting, articulation, etc.); Expressive Language/ Encoding (speaking, writing, spelling); Processing Visual Information
Disability Category:	Attention Deficit/Hyperactivity Disorder

Tactic Title:	**Organizing and Modifying Instruction to Improve Attention**
Problem:	Students with ADHD often have difficulty organizing information and focusing on assigned tasks.
Tactic:	Modify assignments by limiting the number of written responses and monitoring the amount of work completed. First assign the work to the class as a whole. Then give the student a previously prepared, modified version of the work assigned, including a "Work Completion Form" that lists the sections of the work assigned. Modifications to the task may include a reduction in the amount of work assigned, as well as prompts for correct responses. Observe the student and remove distractions if necessary. At the conclusion of the activity, review the student's work with the student and complete a "Work Completion Form" that outlines what the student has accomplished and what still needs to be done.
Example:	Providing students with a modified assignment enables them to focus on the specific goals of the lesson. Reinforcement of the assignment on a 1:1 basis also helps individual students to remain on task. I use this tactic in all content areas because it gives students consistency throughout their day. *Carol K., teacher*
Benefits:	Adapting lessons to meet individual needs • clarifies assignments by giving students a visual model of the tasks; • enables students to be more focused and organized; • is appropriate for all content areas and grade levels; and • can be applied across categories of disability.
Literature:	Aber, M. E., Bachman, B., Campbell, P., & O'Malley, G. (1994). Improving instruction in elementary schools. *Teaching Exceptional Children, 26*(3), 42–50.

Chapter 9:   Adjust Presentations

Strategy:	**Provide Varied Instructional Options**
Focus:	Basic Skills
Area:	Reading; Writing; Social Studies; Science
Learning Difference:	Cognition High; Cognition Low; Cognition Mixed; Memory Short-Term; Memory Long-Term; Speaking/Talking; Fine Motor (handwriting, articulation, etc.); Gross Motor (running, walking, etc.); Processing Visual Information; Processing Verbal Information; Receptive Language/Decoding (listening, reading); Expressive Language/Encoding (speaking, writing, spelling)
Disability Category:	Mental Retardation; Specific Learning Disabilities; Multiple Disabilities; Attention Deficit/Hyperactivity Disorder; Visual Impairments; Deafness/Blindness; Gifted and Talented; Traumatic Brain Injury; Hearing Impairments; Second Language Learning Needs; Serious Emotional Disturbance; Speech or Language Impairments; Orthopedic Impairments; Other Health Impairments; Autism
Tactic Title:	**Modifying Instruction and Evaluation to Meet the Needs of Students With Disabilities**
Problem:	When developing a test, teachers need to make sure all students have the opportunity to succeed, particularly those with reading and writing disabilities.
Tactic:	First modify the lessons so that students with reading and writing difficulties can become active participants (e.g., through group discussion, pictorial activities, or other activities that focus less on writing). Then plan individual writing conferences with the students to help them focus their thoughts and assist them with sentence and grammar structure. Teach students how to keep a reflection log to track the mistakes they have made and how they have solved them. In addition, modify tests to keep written responses to a minimum (e.g., group assessments; pictorial exams; or multiple choice, matching , or short answer questions) and read components of the test aloud to the students if needed. Write down oral descriptions given by students as an additional accommodation for students who need it. Finally, remember to praise the students for any attempt to work through the test independently.
Example:	I've always made sure that the ways in which I assess students' learning match instruction. If a student learns best with a little extra time, tasks broken down into smaller parts, or oral responses, I use the same modifications when giving a test. It's not only fair; it's the only way I can obtain accurate data.
	Roberto S., teacher

Benefits:	Aligning instruction and assessment methods
	• accurately monitors and measures student learning;
	• focuses on student abilities and provides opportunities for success; and
	• is applicable across grade levels, content areas, categories of disability, and learning differences.
Literature:	Giordano, G. (1984). Analyzing and remediating writing disabilities. *Journal of Learning Disabilities, 17,* 78–83.

Chapter 9:   Adjust Presentations

Strategy:	**Alter Pace**
Focus:	Basic Skills
Area:	Reading
Learning Difference:	Attention; Cognition Mixed; Memory Short-Term; Processing Visual Information; Receptive Language/Decoding (listening, reading); Expressive Language/Encoding (speaking, writing, spelling)
Disability Category:	Specific Learning Disabilities

Tactic Title:	**Improving Reading Rate and Comprehension**
Problem:	Teachers often find that students with specific learning disabilities need extra practice to improve their reading rate and comprehension.
Tactic:	Present students with reading passages on a computer. Many computers and word processing programs are design to accommodate different reading rates. The passage appears line by line at an initial preset speed. Students read the passage aloud, then stop and answer questions based on the content of what they just read. If students answer all or most of the questions correctly, increase the speed of the appearance of the next passage on the computer. If they do not answer all or most of the questions correctly, the students should continue reading at the same speed until they have mastered reading and comprehending at that pace. Continue this procedure until students achieve the desired amount of practice and speed.
Example:	I use a "read aloud" program in which the computer reads the text to the student. This allows the student to receive auditory input, which may be an effective strategy for students who have good auditory comprehension. Visual aids to go along with stories on the computers are also productive to meet the needs of different learning styles. I also tape-record my students when they are reading orally. I can review the tapes later and keep a record of their rate and accuracy. Their tapes become part of their portfolios and demonstrate clearly their progress over time . . . a great tool for student and parent conferences.
	Stacy R., teacher
Benefits:	Using technology to alter the pace of instruction • is an easy and effective way to improve reading speed and comprehension; • can be modified to fit the specific age, grade, or interests; and • can make reading more interesting and meaningful.
Literature:	Montali, J., & Lewandowski, L. (1996). Bimodal reading: Benefits of a talking computer for average and less skilled readers. *Journal of Learning Disabilities, 29,* 271–279.

Evaluating Instruction

Effective teachers continuously monitor their students' understanding of the content being presented. They also monitor their students' use of instructional time to maximize the time they spend actively engaged in appropriate learning activities. They keep records of progress and use the data to make decisions. In this part, we describe evidence-based strategies for each principle of evaluating instruction.

Component	Principle	Strategy
Evaluating Instruction (Part IV)	Monitor Student Understanding (Chapter 10)	Check Understanding of Directions
		Check Procedural Understanding
		Monitor Student Success Rate
	Monitor Engaged Time (Chapter 11)	Check Student Participation
		Teach Students to Monitor Their Own Participation
	Keep Records of Student Progress (Chapter 12)	Teach Students to Chart Their Own Progress
		Regularly Inform Students of Performance
		Maintain Records of Student Performance
	Use Data to Make Decisions (Chapter 13)	Use Data to Decide If More Services Are Warranted
		Use Student Progress to Make Teaching Decisions
		Use Student Progress to Decide When to Discontinue Service

Evaluating Instruction Works: A Case Study

I teach second grade at Paradise Elementary. This year, I have four students with disabilities in my class—two with learning disabilities, one with Down syndrome, and one with cerebral palsy. Then there are several others who are simply struggling with reading. I know it's important to monitor my students' learning, but I've been unsure as to how to do it well with such a diverse group of learners.

I found the tactic "Celebrating Reading" so helpful. It only takes a few minutes each day, but it tells me where my students are and I can use that information to plan for the next day or two. Also, given that we are supposed to be using "evidenced-based" practices, it is reassuring to know that this tactic is supported in the literature and has been successful in other settings. (Related tactic is located in Chapter 13: Use Data to Make Decisions under Strategy: Use Student Progress to Make Teaching Decisions.)

10

Monitor Student Understanding

Component	Principle	Strategy
Evaluating Instruction	Monitor Student Understanding	Check Understanding of Directions
		Check Procedural Understanding
		Monitor Student Success Rate

Chapter 10:   Monitor Student Understanding

Strategy:	**Check Understanding of Directions**
Focus:	Basic Skills
Area:	Reading; Mathematics/Problem Solving/Calculating; Social Studies; Science; Arts; Fitness
Learning Difference:	Attention; Memory Short-Term; Memory Long-Term; Processing Verbal Information; Receptive Language/Decoding (listening, reading)
Disability Category:	Specific Learning Disabilities; Second Language Learning Needs; Speech or Language Impairments

Tactic Title:	**Make Students Repeat Directions in Their Own Words**
Problem:	Many students have difficulty following directions because they either have trouble listening to and processing verbal information or simply do not understand the directions.
Tactic:	After giving students a set of directions, simply ask several students to repeat the directions in their own words. Correct misinterpretations immediately. Posting the directions is also reinforcing.
Example:	I use this tactic whenever I am giving instructions to large and small groups and especially when I am teaching a student individually. I do not want my students to practice errors or waste time because they do not understand what they are to do. For some students, I provide individual directions that are broken down into smaller parts. That really seems to help them monitor their learning as they check off each smaller component of their work.
	Taisha N., teacher
Benefits:	By checking for understanding,
	• teachers know if individual students have listened to, processed, and understood directions;
	• students can affirm their own understanding of instructions by listening to the words of their peers; and
	• teachers can follow up with learners who may need more individualized instructions.
Literature:	Batshaw, M. L. (1997). *Children with disabilities* (4th ed.). Baltimore, MD: Brookes.

Chapter 10:   Monitor Student Understanding

Strategy:	Check Procedural Understanding
Focus:	Basic Skills
Area:	Reading; Mathematics/Problem Solving/Calculating; Writing; Social Studies; Science; Arts; Fitness
Learning Difference:	Attention; Cognition Mixed; Memory Short-Term; Study Skills; Processing Verbal Information; Receptive Language/Decoding (listening, reading); Self-Control; Social Behaviors; Self-Confidence
Disability Category:	Specific Learning Disabilities; Attention Deficit/Hyperactivity Disorder

Tactic Title:	Step-by-Step Instructions
Problem:	Often, teachers give the students all the steps required to complete an activity before they have started the activity. This is fine for students with strong recall skills but not for students with poor short-term recall or attention deficits.
Tactic:	Instead of overloading the students with all the steps, provide instructions one step at a time. For a student to proceed to the next step, the student must complete the preceding step. With primary-age students, the teacher can exchange colored index cards that describe one direction per card.
Example:	For my students who struggle with following directions, I provide individual checklists on 4 × 6 inch index cards that they tape to their desks. As they complete each small step, they check it off and can go on to the next step. This really helps my paraprofessional, my special education coteacher, the student, and me monitor learning throughout an activity. We are able to scan the room easily and provide immediate assistance/reassurance wherever needed.
	Rodney P., teacher
Benefits:	Breaking procedures into smaller manageable steps
	• ensures that students are not overwhelmed by the number of steps needed to complete a task;
	• enables students to focus on the current task and not be distracted by trying to remember what to do next; and
	• is a useful tactic across content areas, grade levels, categories of disabilities, and settings.
Literature:	Shenkle, A. M. (1989). Orchestrating the words. *Learning, 17*(5), 40–41.

Chapter 10:   Monitor Student Understanding

Strategy:	**Monitor Student Success Rate**
Focus:	Basic Skills
Area:	Reading; Mathematics/Problem Solving/Calculating; Writing; Social Studies; Science; Arts; Fitness
Learning Difference:	Cognition Mixed; Attention; Memory Long-Term; Memory Short-Term; Cognition Low; Cognition High; Receptive Language/Decoding (listening, reading); Expressive Language/Encoding (speaking, writing, spelling); Study Skills; Fine Motor (handwriting, articulation, etc.); Processing Visual Information; Self-Control; Processing Verbal Information; Social Behaviors; Self-Confidence; Self-Care
Disability Category:	Specific Learning Disabilities; Visual Impairments; Deafness/Blindness; Gifted and Talented; Hearing Impairments; Mental Retardation; Multiple Disabilities; Traumatic Brain Injury; Second Language Learning Needs; Serious Emotional Disturbance; Speech or Language Impairments; Attention Deficit/Hyperactivity Disorder; Orthopedic Impairments; Other Health Impairments; Autism

Tactic Title:	**Alternative Assessment**
Problem:	It is very frustrating for students and their parents when report cards do not report/reflect progress.
Tactic:	Throughout the school year, collect the student's work in a portfolio. Allow the student to separate a few pieces of work that exemplify progress. The student should write about why the items were selected and how they show growth. Grade the student on improvement rather than content over an extended period of time. If that is not possible, then provide additional information from the portfolio.
Example:	My students select the contents of their portfolios; they must provide a rationale for each piece they select. I meet with them regularly to review their portfolios and have a conversation about their learning. Then during parent conferences, my students and I present the portfolios, as well as the formal reports, and discuss the items and what they represent. Even though my school district's policy forces me to grade my students according to grade-level standards, my students and I can provide evidence of their individual growth. *Nancy S., teacher*
Benefits:	Portfolios • provide teachers with alternative ways to show evidence of student learning;

- can engage teachers, students, and parents in the evaluation process;
- provide essential information to supplement letter grades; and
- can document student progress toward meeting IEP goals and objectives.

Literature: Munk, D. D., & Bursuck, W. D. (1998). Can grades be helpful and fair? *Educational Leadership, 55,* 44.

11

Monitor Engaged Time

Component	Principle	Strategy
Evaluating Instruction	Monitor Engaged Time	Check Student Participation
		Teach Students to Monitor Their Own Participation

Chapter 11:   Monitor Engaged Time

Strategy:	**Check Student Participation**
Focus:	Basic Skills
Area:	Reading; Mathematics/Problem Solving/Calculating; Writing; Social Studies; Science
Learning Difference:	Attention; Cognition Low; Processing Visual Information; Processing Verbal Information; Receptive Language/Decoding (listening, reading); Expressive Language/Encoding (speaking, writing, spelling); Self-Control
Disability Category:	Attention Deficit/Hyperactivity Disorder; Speech or Language Impairments; Specific Learning Disabilities; Serious Emotional Disturbance; Second Language Learning Needs; Autism; Traumatic Brain Injury; Mental Retardation

Tactic Title:	**Putting the Pieces Together**
Problem:	For many students, remaining on-task during instruction can be challenging.
Tactic:	First provide students with an outline of the same animal. Then have them decorate their animal individually. Students next cut off each limb (i.e., the legs, arms, head, and body). Attach the body of the object to the desk with tape. Post the large "teacher" version where it is visible to all students. During a lesson, randomly attach different body parts to the body of the teacher animal. When students notice that the teacher has added a body part, they add the same body part to their own animal on their desk. By the end of the lesson, the object on each student's desk should be identical to the one on the board.
Example:	This is an excellent way to "see" if all students are following along by simply scanning the students' desks. I usually ask students to make sure their classmates are on track by silently pointing to the added body part. Some of my more artistic students love to help in designing new animals or other objects for our learning puzzles. I love this tactic because it requires no verbal cues, does not interrupt instruction, yet keeps students on task.

Cecelia W., teacher

Benefits:	Monitoring instruction while working with students

- is an easy way to determine visually if students are on-task and paying attention;

- enables paraprofessionals, peers, or other teachers to provide guidance; and
- makes learning fun.

Literature: Kemp, K., Fister, S., & McLaughlin, P. J. (1995). Academic strategies for children with ADD. *Intervention in School and Clinic, 30*(4), 203–210.

Chapter 11:   Monitor Engaged Time

Strategy:	**Teach Students to Monitor Their Own Participation**

Focus: Basic Skills

Area: Reading; Mathematics/Problem Solving/Calculating; Writing; Social Studies; Science

Learning Difference: Attention; Cognition Mixed; Memory Short-Term; Memory Long-Term; Receptive Language/Decoding (listening, reading); Self-Control; Social Behaviors; Self-Confidence

Disability Category: Attention Deficit/Hyperactivity Disorder

Tactic Title:	**Self-Monitoring With a Tape Recorder**

Problem: It is often difficult for students with learning differences to remain on-task.

Tactic: One way to help students remain on-task is to institute a self-monitoring program. Using a blank audiocassette, record a tone after every five to ten minutes of silence. Place a small tape player with this tape and headphones on the student's desk during individual seatwork time. Provide the student with a chart titled "Was I Paying Attention?" The chart provides several opportunities for the student to record a yes or no response. Explain to the student that a tone will ring every five to ten minutes. When the student hears the tone, the student should ask: "Am I on-task?" and make the appropriate mark on the chart. At the end of the day, total the yes and no responses and provide the appropriate reward for on-task behavior.

Example: I love this strategy. It is individualized; it doesn't disturb the learning of others; and it works! It doesn't matter if students are totally truthful in the beginning. The important thing is, they are paying attention to paying attention. I build in a teacher-student agreement factor if I suspect there is less than total honesty. Both the student and I rate the behavior, and the student earns points when we are in agreement. I adjust the intervals between the tones as on-task behavior changes.

Charlie F., teacher

Benefits: Self monitoring strategies
- remind students constantly to think about being on-task;
- teach students to take responsibility for monitoring and controlling their own behavior; and
- teach students to stay on-task.

Literature: Corral, N., & Antia, S. D. (1997). Self-talk: Strategies for success in math. *Teaching Exceptional Children, 29,* 42–45.

12

Keep Records of Student Progress

Component	Principle	Strategy
Evaluating Instruction	Keep Records of Student Progress	Teach Students to Chart Their Own Progress
		Regularly Inform Students of Performance
		Maintain Records of Student Performance

Chapter 12:   Keep Records of Student Progress

Strategy:	**Teach Students to Chart Their Own Progress**
Focus:	Basic Skills
Area:	Reading; Mathematics/Problem Solving/Calculating; Writing; Social Studies; Science; Arts; Fitness
Learning Difference:	Attention; Study Skills; Processing Verbal Information; Receptive Language/Decoding (listening, reading); Self-Control; Social Behaviors; Self-Confidence
Disability Category:	Speech or Language Impairments; Autism

Tactic Title:	**Using Instructional Checklists**
Problem:	Frequently, students who have difficulty maintaining their attention do not listen to instructions or monitor their behavior during academic tasks. As a result, they become frustrated and begin to display disruptive behavior when they are unsure of the sequential steps needed to complete an assignment.
Tactic:	Provide students with instructional checklists and show students how to use them to help maintain and chart their own academic progress. As students listen to the teacher's directions, they follow along and check off each instructional step on the checklist. The checklist provides the students with prompts that guide them through the assignment or project. As students complete the task, it is checked off, allowing them to record their own academic progress. When the allotted time has expired, students circle the tasks they have not completed. The circled items then become a homework checklist.
Example:	Teaching students to use a checklist has improved their attending skills and provided them with a visual representation of the work they have completed and the work that remains undone. By monitoring their own progress, they have learned to complete assignments independently and be positively reinforced for completing tasks. As a result, disruptive behavior has decreased and the amount of completed work has increased. *Sam S., teacher*
Benefits:	Instructional checklists • can be used with a broad range of students with special needs across content areas and grade levels; • are a wonderful tool to enhance communication among teachers, students, and parents; and • teach students to take responsibility for their learning.
Literature:	Farrow, L. (1996). A quartet of success stories: How to make inclusion work. *Educational Leadership, 53*(5), 51–55.

Chapter 12:   Keep Records of Student Progress

Strategy:	**Regularly Inform Students of Performance**
Focus:	Basic Skills
Area:	Reading; Mathematics/Problem Solving/Calculating; Writing; Social Studies; Science; Arts; Fitness
Learning Difference:	Attention; Fine Motor (handwriting, articulation, etc.); Processing Visual Information; Processing Verbal Information; Receptive Language/Decoding (listening, reading); Self-Control
Disability Category:	Deafness/Blindness; Gifted and Talented; Visual Impairments; Hearing Impairments; Mental Retardation; Multiple Disabilities; Traumatic Brain Injury; Second Language Learning Needs; Serious Emotional Disturbance; Speech or Language Impairments; Specific Learning Disabilities; Attention Deficit/Hyperactivity Disorder; Orthopedic Impairments; Other Health Impairments; Autism

Tactic Title:	**Assessing Students With Diverse Learning Needs**
Problem:	Ongoing communication with students regarding their learning is essential.
Tactic:	Clearly define what is to be measured. Use a rubric to show how the student will be evaluated (e.g., Exceeds Expectations, Meets Expectations, Fails to Meet Expectations). Provide clear criteria for each category. Be consistent and objective. Create a chart for each student to show progress toward goals. The chart should contain the activity, the objectives, and the level of achievement.
Example:	I have found rubrics to be so helpful in keeping my students informed as to their performance. I use them during individual conferences with my students and also during parent conferences. Students maintain their own charts and really like being able to "see" their progress. It helps them strategize and prioritize. I truly believe that having this information promotes their continued growth. Some of my students are now learning to use the rubrics to assess their work themselves.
	Susan R., teacher
Benefits:	Rubrics and visual records of learning

- enable students and their parents to see their accomplishments;
- set clear expectations for progress;
- allow students to see both their strengths and their weaknesses; and
- teach students to accept greater responsibility for their learning.

Literature: Stauffer, S. L. (1999). Beginning assessment in elementary general music. *Music Educators Journal, 86,* 25–30.

Stevens, D. D., & Levi, A. J. (2004). *Introduction to rubrics: An assessment tool to save grading time, convey effective feedback and promote student learning.* Sterling, VA: Stylus.

Chapter 12: Keep Records of Student Progress

Strategy:	**Maintain Records of Student Performance**

Focus: Basic Skills

Area: Reading; Mathematics/Problem Solving/Calculating; Writing; Social Studies; Science

Learning Difference: Processing Visual Information; Receptive Language/Decoding (listening, reading); Processing Verbal Information; Expressive Language/Encoding (speaking, writing, spelling); Cognition High; Cognition Low; Cognition Mixed; Fine Motor (handwriting, articulation, etc.)

Disability Category: Specific Learning Disabilities; Attention Deficit Disorder; Visual Impairments; Deafness/Blindness; Gifted and Talented; Hearing Impairments; Mental Retardation; Multiple Disabilities; Traumatic Brain Injury; Second Language Learning Needs; Serious Emotional Disturbance; Speech or Language Impairments; Attention Deficit/ Hyperactivity Disorder; Orthopedic Impairments; Other Health Impairments; Autism

Tactic Title:	**Using a Standards-Based Grading System**

Problem: Teachers often find that moving toward standards-based education means they can no longer use a traditional grade book to record student progress. The traditional system is efficient when grading simply involves calculating percentages on tests and adding class participation marks to determine a final grade. However, when teachers begin to assess students on curriculum standards and must report student progress in relation to the standards, a new, improved standards-based grading system must be utilized.

Tactic: First create a new grade book that uses one page for each student, with curriculum standards for each subject on the left and a grid on the right for marking scores. Next designate symbols for performance, assessment, assignment, direct observation, and percentage of correct answers. Then develop a mark system (plus, check, minus) to note students' levels of performance. Finally, create a color system to designate time periods of the assessments.

Example: We all know that standardized and mandated tests do not really measure the learning of all students, especially those with Individualized Educational Programs. Their annual goals and objectives are typically not aligned with the state grade-level standards. So they are "punished" because their individual programs are in conflict with their grade-level standards. I've really struggled to find a clear, organized way to maintain accurate and informative records of my students' learning so they and their parents are not "defeated" by the mandated grading system. Using this tactic has been a lifesaver!

Eddie S., teacher

Benefits: Maintaining detailed and informative records of student learning

- works for assessing all students but especially those with IEPs;
- clearly shows how well students are progressing in relation to each standard;
- tells teachers where students still need additional support; and
- makes teaching easier.

Literature: Salend, S. J. (2005). Report card models that support communication and differentiation of instruction. *Teaching Exceptional Children, 37*(4), 28–34.

13

Use Data to Make Decisions

Component	Principle	Strategy
Evaluating Instruction	Use Data to Make Decisions	Use Data to Decide If More Services Are Warranted
		Use Student Progress to Make Teaching Decisions
		Use Student Progress to Decide When to Discontinue Service

Chapter 13:   Use Data to Make Decisions

Strategy:	**Use Data to Decide If More Services Are Warranted**
Focus:	Basic Skills
Area:	Reading; Mathematics/Problem Solving/Calculating; Writing; Social Studies; Science; Arts; Fitness
Learning Difference:	Attention; Self-Control; Social Behaviors
Disability Category:	Serious Emotional Disturbance

Tactic Title:	**Professional Conversations About Student Performance**
Problem:	New students, particularly those with serious emotional disturbance (SED), often need assistance in adjusting to a new environment.
Tactic:	Communication among professionals within the school is essential in dealing with students showing characteristics of SED. For this reason, the teachers, paraprofessionals, school psychologist, reading specialist, special education teacher, and others work cooperatively to determine the best ways to help students learn. Meet on a regular basis to discuss students' behaviors, difficulties, and improvements. Take this opportunity to modify teaching strategies to ensure that they are as productive and appropriate as possible. Take into account any progress the student has made and adjust teaching tactics in areas where the student is not improving. Monitor progress to decide if additional services are warranted.
Example:	Elias is new to our classroom. His family just moved to our district, and this is his fourth school in two years. He's been struggling in adapting to our routines and procedures, and as a result, his learning is at a standstill. I've been keeping data on his behavior and meeting with his special education teacher and the school counselor regularly. We've decided that he would benefit from small-group sessions with our counselor. She uses chess to teach students strategies for succeeding and dealing with loss. So we're meeting with his parents this afternoon to modify his IEP.
	Wendy H., teacher
Benefits:	Using data to make collaborative decisions
	• can prevent problems from escalating;
	• may indicate any discrepancies in behavior across teachers and settings;
	• fosters maintenance and generalization of appropriate behaviors;
	• ensures consistency for the student across people, times, and settings; and
	• supports students at varying levels of ability.
Literature:	Schlichter, C., & Brown, V. (1985). Application of the Renzulli Model for the education of the gifted and talented to other categories of special education. *Remedial and Special Education, 6,* 49–55.

Chapter 13:   Use Data to Make Decisions

Strategy:	**Use Student Progress to Make Teaching Decisions**
Focus:	Basic Skills
Area:	Reading
Learning Difference:	Speaking/Talking; Receptive Language/Decoding (listening, reading); Self-Confidence; Memory Short-Term; Memory Long-Term; Processing Visual Information; Processing Verbal Information; Expressive Language/ Encoding (speaking, writing, spelling)
Disability Category:	Specific Learning Disabilities; Visual Impairments; Deafness/Blindness; Hearing Impairments; Mental Retardation; Traumatic Brain Injury; Second Language Learning Needs; Serious Emotional Disturbance; Speech or Language Impairments; Attention Deficit/Hyperactivity Disorder; Autism

Title:	**Celebrating Reading**
Problem:	To establish a positive classroom environment and monitor student performance during reading, students can celebrate their accomplishments in reading.
Tactic:	At the end of reading each day, randomly select two students to share a passage orally. Note strengths and weaknesses of their reading. Use these notations to determine how to help the students become stronger readers. For example, the teacher may note that a student repeatedly leaves the endings off words. With these notations, the teacher is able to individualize subsequent instruction. At the end of each reading, regardless of student performance, the student receives a certificate and is acknowledged on a bulletin board display.
Example:	On Friday afternoons, we have a special class meeting where we talk about what we've accomplished, as well as any issues that we have faced during the week. I also give out awards to the Most Improved Reader, Mathematician, Scientist, the Best Friend, etc. Then, one student is selected as the Star of the Week. I use my notes from the mini-celebrations during the week not only to make teaching decisions but also to determine the winners. All winners receive "official" certificates, and their names and photographs are posted on the bulletin board in the hall. My students have learned that being the "best" is not always possible, but everyone can improve. I believe this public celebration is so important. *Xinia F., teacher*
Benefits:	Keeping ongoing anecdotal data regarding public student performances • is an effective strategy for monitoring student progress while maintaining a positive environment; • enables teachers to make informed decisions about student strengths and needs;

- ensures that students are never penalized or criticized;
- teaches students to be supportive of one another's efforts and to appreciate the accomplishments of their classmates; and
- creates a safe place to share learning differences.

Literature: Glazer, S. M. (1998). Encouraging remarks. *Teaching PreK–8, 29,* 124–126.

Chapter 13:   Use Data to Make Decisions

Strategy:	**Use Student Progress to Decide When to Discontinue Service**
Focus:	Basic Skills
Area:	Reading; Mathematics/Problem Solving/Calculating; Writing; Social Studies; Science; Arts; Fitness
Learning Difference:	Attention; Speaking/Talking; Fine Motor (handwriting, articulation, etc.); Receptive Language/Decoding (listening, reading); Expressive Language/Encoding (speaking, writing, spelling); Social Knowledge; Self-Control; Social Behaviors
Disability Category:	Specific Learning Disabilities; Attention Deficit Disorder; Attention Deficit/Hyperactivity Disorder; Hearing Impairments; Speech or Language Impairments

Tactic Title:	**Recording Observations of Student Progress**
Problem:	Teachers are often required to provide data on the progress of students with special needs. Besides providing student products and testing information, it is beneficial to provide data obtained through observations of students.
Tactic:	Whenever there is an opportunity to observe a student, have paper and pencil handy with which to write pertinent notes of observed student behavior. This might be a logbook or something as informal as Post-it® Notes or scraps of paper. The idea is to jot down the observation that you feel is useful information about the student's progress while it is fresh in your mind. Strengths, accomplishments, and needs can be quickly noted. The notes can later be transferred to the student's individual file.
Example:	Ms. Cox and I have kept anecdotal observational data on several students with special needs in our classroom. In Jamie's case, that information was the key in helping the IEP team decide that he no longer needed special education services. He has learned to make appropriate accommodations for himself and be his own best advocate with his teachers. His parents are delighted with his progress and totally agree with the decision.

Curt R., teacher

Benefits:	Keeping observational data and maintaining accurate records of student performance

- enables teachers to have accurate, pertinent information about a student's progress;

- provides data for parent conferences, student conferences, and IEP teams; and
- becomes even more powerful when all teachers in the student's day record their observations.

Literature: Hankins, K. H. (1998). Cacophony to symphony: Memoirs in teacher research. *Harvard Educational Review. 68*(1), 80–95.

References

Aber, M. E., Bachman, B., Campbell, P., & O'Malley, G. (1994). Improving instruction in elementary schools. *Teaching Exceptional Children, 26*(3), 42–50.

Algozzine, B., & Ysseldyke, J. E. (1992). *Strategies and tactics for effective instruction.* Longmont, CO: Sopris West.

Algozzine, B., Ysseldyke, J., & Elliott, J. (1997). *Strategies and tactics for effective instruction.* Longmont, CO: Sopris West.

AlphaSmart Direct Inc. (2008). *AlphaSmart™.* Retrieved January 6, 2008, from http://www.alphasmart.com

Anderson, L. W., & Krathwohl, D. R. (Eds.). (2001). *A taxonomy for learning, teaching, and assessing: A revision of Bloom's taxonomy of educational objectives* (abridged). New York: Longman.

Armstrong, D. C. (1994). Gifted child's education requires real dialogue: The use of interactive writing for collaborative education. *Gifted Child Quarterly, 38,* 136–145.

Arreaga-Mayer, C. (1998). Increasing active student responding and improving academic performance through classwide peer tutoring. *Intervention in School and Clinic, 34,* 89–94.

Batshaw, M. L. (1997). *Children with disabilities* (4th ed.). Baltimore, MD: Brookes.

Bolocofsky, D. N. (1980). Motivational effects of classroom competition as a function of field dependence. *Journal of Educational Research, 73,* 213–217.

Bonus, M., & Riordan, L. (1998). *Increasing student on-task behavior through the use of specific seating arrangements* (Master's Action Research Project). Chicago: Saint Xavier University. (ERIC Document Reproduction Service No. ED422129)

Burns, M. S., Delclos, V. R., & Kulewicz, S. J. (1987). Effects of dynamic assessment on teachers' expectations of handicapped children. *American Educational Research Journal, 24,* 325–336.

Campbell, P., & Siperstein, G. N. (1994). *Improving social competence: A resource for elementary school teachers.* Boston: Allyn & Bacon.

Charney, R. S. (2002). *Teaching children to care: Classroom management for ethical and academic growth, K–8* (rev. ed.). Turners Falls, MA: Northeast Foundation for Children.

Clarke-Klein, S. M. (1994). Expressive phonological deficiencies: Impact on spelling development. *Topics in Language Disorders, 14,* 40.

Cohen, M. (1993). Machines for thinking: The computer's role in schools. *Educational and Training Technology International, 30,* 57.

Corral, N., & Antia, S. D. (1997). Self-talk: Strategies for success in math. *Teaching Exceptional Children, 29,* 42–45.

Crozier, S., & Tincani, M. J. (2005). Using a modified social story to decrease disruptive behavior of a child with autism. *Focus on Autism and Other Developmental Disabilities, 20,* 150–157.

de l'Etoile, S. (1996). Meeting the needs of the special learner in music. *American Music Teacher, 45,* 10–13.

Dollard, N., & Christensen, L. (1996). Constructive classroom management. *Focus on Exceptional Children, 29,* 1–11.

Dowd, J. (1997). Refusing to play the blame game. *Educational Leadership, 54,* 67–69.

Duffy-Hester, A. (1999). Teaching struggling readers in elementary school classrooms: A review of classroom reading programs and principles for instruction. *The Reading Teacher, 52,* 480–495.

Eakin, S., & Douglas, V. (1971). Automatization and oral reading problems in children. *Journal of Learning Disabilities, 4,* 31–38.

Epstein, T., & Elias, M. (1996). To reach for the stars: How social/affective education can foster truly inclusive environments. *Phi Delta Kappan, 78*, 157–163.

Farrow, L. (1996). A quartet of success stories: How to make inclusion work. *Educational Leadership, 53*(5), 51–55.

Fleischner, J. E., & Manheimer, M. A. (1997). Math interventions for students with learning disabilities: Myths and realities. *School Psychology Review, 26*, 397–413.

Friar, K. K. (1999). Changing voices, changing times. *Music Educators Journal, 86*, 26–29.

Gallas, K. (1991). Arts as epistemology: Enabling children to know what they know. *Harvard Educational Review, 61*, 93–105.

Gardill, M. C., DuPaul, G. J., & Kyle, K. E. (1996). Classroom strategies for managing students with attention-deficit/hyperactivity disorder. *Intervention in School and Clinic, 32*, 89–94.

Geocaris, C., & Ross, M. (1999). A test worth taking. *Educational Leadership, 57*(1), 29–33.

Giordano, G. (1984). Analyzing and remediating writing disabilities. *Journal of Learning Disabilities, 17*, 78–83.

Glazer, S. M. (1998). Encouraging remarks. *Teaching PreK–8, 29*, 124–126.

Goolsby, T. W. (1999). Assessment in instrumental music. *Music Educators Journal, 95*, 31.

Graham, S., & Harris, K. R. (2006). Preventing writing difficulties: Providing additional handwriting and spelling instruction to at-risk children in first grade. *Teaching Exceptional Children, 38*(5), 64–66.

Graves, M., & Graves, B. (1996). Scaffolding reading experiences for inclusive classes. *Educational Leadership, 53*(5), 14–16.

Gunter, P. L., Denny, R. K., Jack, S. L., Shores, R. E., & Nelson, C. M. (1993). Aversive stimuli in academic interactions between students with serious emotional disturbance and their teachers. *Behavioral Disorders, 18*, 265.

Hankins, K. H. (1998). Cacophony to symphony: Memoirs in teacher research. *Harvard Educational Review, 68*(1), 80–95.

Harris, K. C., & Nevin, A. (1994). Developing and using collaborative bilingual special education teams. In Lilliam M. Malave (Ed.), *Annual Conference Journal, NABE '92–'93* (pp. 25–35). Washington, DC: National Association for Bilingual Education. (ERIC Document Reproduction Service No. ED372643)

Higdon, H. (1999). Getting their attention. *Runner's World, 34*, 84.

Johnson, L., Graham, S., & Harris, K. R. (1997). The effects of goal setting and self-instruction on learning a reading comprehension strategy: A study of students with learning disabilities. *Journal of Learning Disabilities, 30*, 80–91.

Kemp, S., Fister, S., & McLaughlin, P. J. (1995). Academic strategies for children with ADD. *Intervention in School and Clinic, 30*(4), 203–210.

Kroeger, S. D., & Kouche, B. (2006). Using peer-assisted learning strategies to increase response to intervention in inclusive middle math settings. *Teaching Exceptional Children, 38*(5), 6–13.

Levy, N. R. (1996). Classroom strategies for managing students with attention-deficit/hyperactivity disorder. *Intervention in School and Clinic, 32*(2), 89–94.

Lewis, R. B. (1998). Assistive technology and learning disabilities: Today's realities and tomorrow's promises. *Journal of Learning Disabilities, 31*, 16–26.

Macy, M. G., & Bricker, D. D. (2007). Embedding individualized social goals into routine activities in inclusive early childhood classrooms. *Early Child Development & Care, 177*, 107–120.

Martens, P. (1998). Using retrospective miscue analysis to inquire: Learning from Michael. *The Reading Teacher, 52*, 176–180.

Marzano, R. J., Pickering, D. J., & Pollack, J. E. (2003). *Classroom instruction that works: Research-based strategies for increasing student achievement.* Alexandria, VA: Association for Supervision and Curriculum Development.

Mayer, G. R. (1999). Constructive discipline for school personnel. *Education and Treatment of Children, 22*, 36–54.

McGrail, L. (1998). Modifying regular classroom curricula for high ability students. *Gifted Child Today, 21*(2), 36–39.

Montali, J., & Lewandowski, L. (1996). Bimodal reading: Benefits of a talking computer for average and less skilled readers. *Journal of Learning Disabilities, 29*, 271–279.

Morgan, M., & Moni, K. B. (2007). Motivate students with disabilities using sight-vocabulary activities. *Intervention in School & Clinic, 48,* 229–233.

Munk, D. D., & Bursuck, W. D. (1998). Can grades be helpful and fair? *Educational Leadership, 55,* 44.

Murphy, D. M. (1996). Implications of inclusion for general and special education. *The Elementary School Journal, 96,* 469–493.

Niebling, B. C., & Elliott, S. N. (2005). Testing accommodations and inclusive assessment practices. *Assessment for Effective Intervention, 31*(1), 1–6.

Prater, M. A. (1992). Increasing time-on-task in the classroom. *Intervention in School and Clinic, 28*(1), 22–27.

Rhizzo, T., Faison-Hodge, J., Woodard, R., & Sayers, K. (2003). Factors affecting social experiences in inclusive physical education. *Adapted Physical Activity Quarterly, 20*(3), 317.

Roberson, T. (1984). Determining curriculum content for the gifted. *Roeper Review, 6,* 137–139.

Ruth, W. J. (1996). Goal setting and behavior contracting for students with emotional and behavioral difficulties. *Psychology in the Schools, 33,* 153–158.

Saarimaki, P. (1995). Math in your world. *National Council of Teachers of Mathematics, 9,* 565–569.

Salend, S. J. (2005). Report card models that support communication and differentiation of instruction. *Teaching Exceptional Children, 37*(4), 28–34.

Schirmer, B. R. (1987). Boosting reading success. *Teaching Exceptional Children, 30*(1), 52–55.

Schlichter, C., & Brown, V. (1985). Application of the Renzulli Model for the education of the gifted and talented to other categories of special education. *Remedial and Special Education, 6,* 49–55.

Shaaban, K. (2006). An initial study of the effects of cooperative learning on reading comprehension, vocabulary acquisition, and motivation to read. *Reading Psychology, 27,* 377–403.

Shenkle, A. M. (1989). Orchestrating the words. *Learning, 17*(5), 40–41.

Sprouse, C. A., Hall, C. W., Webster, R. E., & Bolen, L. M. (1998). Social perception in students with learning disabilities and attention deficit/hyperactivity disorder. *Journal of Nonverbal Behavior, 22,* 125–134.

Stauffer, S. L. (1999). Beginning assessment in elementary general music. *Music Educators Journal, 86,* 25–30.

Stevens, D. D., & Levi, A. J. (2004). *Introduction to rubrics: An assessment tool to save grading time, convey effective feedback and promote student learning.* Sterling, VA: Stylus.

Stormont-Spurgin, M. (1997). I lost my homework: Strategies for improving organization in students with ADHD. *Intervention in School and Clinic, 32,* 270–274.

Swanson, P. (1998). Teaching effective comprehension strategies to students with learning and reading disabilities. *Intervention in School and Clinic, 33,* 209–218.

Tomlinson, C. A. (2004). *The differentiated classroom: Responding to the needs of all learners.* Upper Saddle River, NJ: Prentice-Hall.

Vaughn, S., Hughes, M. T., Schumm, J. S., & Klingner, J. (1998). A collaborative effort to enhance reading and writing instruction in inclusion classrooms. *Learning Disabilities Quarterly, 21,* 57–74.

Willis, S. (1996). Managing today's classroom: Finding alternatives to control and compliance. *Education Update* (Newsletter of the Association for Supervision and Curriculum Development), *38*(6), 1, 3–7.

Wirtz, C. L., Gardner III, R., Weber, K., & Bullara, D. (1996). Using self-correction to improve the spelling performance of low-achieving third graders. *Remedial and Special Education, 17,* 48–58.

Zadnik, D. (1992). *Instructional supervision in special education: Integrating teacher effectiveness research into model supervisory practices.* Bloomington: Indiana University, School of Education and Council of Administrators of Special Education. (ERIC Document Reproduction Service No. ED358646)

Additional Readings

Abbott, M., Walton, C., & Greenwood, C. R. (2002). Phonemic awareness in kindergarten and first grade. *Teaching Exceptional Children, 34*(4), 20–26.

Allsopp, D. H. (1997). Using classwide peer tutoring to teach beginning algebra problem solving skills in heterogeneous classrooms. *Remedial and Special Education, 18,* 367–379.

Behrmann, M. M. (1994). Assistive technology for students with mild disabilities. *Intervention in School and Clinic, 30*(2), 70–82.

Beirne-Smith, M. (1991). Peer tutoring in arithmetic for children with learning disabilities. *Exceptional Children, 57,* 330.

Belfiore, P. J., Grskovic, J. A., Murphy, A. M., & Zentall, S. S. (1996). The effects of antecedent color on reading for students with learning disabilities and co-occurring attention-deficit/hyperactivity disorder. *Journal of Learning Disabilities, 29,* 432–438.

Bergman, A. B. (1993). Performance assessment for early childhood. *Science and Children, 30*(5), 20–22.

Bernstorf, E. D., & Welsbacher, B. T. (1996). Helping students in the inclusive classroom. *Music Educators Journal, 82,* 21–37.

Birenbaum, M., & Feldman, R. A. (1998). Relationships between learning patterns and attitudes toward two assessment formats. *Educational Research, 40,* 90.

Bos, C. S., Mather, N., Silver-Pacuilla, H., & Narr, R. F. (2000). Learning to teach early literacy skills—Collaboratively. *Teaching Exceptional Children, 32*(5), 38–45.

Boulineau, T., Fore III, C., Hagan-Burke, S., & Burke, M. D. (2004). Use of story-mapping to increase the story-grammar text comprehension of elementary students with learning disabilities. *Learning Disability Quarterly, 27,* 105–120.

Bower, B. (1989). Remodeling the autistic child. *Science News, 136,* 312–313.

Bromley, K., & Mannix, D. (1993). Beyond the classroom: Publishing student work in magazines. *Reading Teacher, 47,* 72–77.

Browder, D. M., Wakeman, S. Y., Spooner, F., Ahlgrim-Delzell, L., & Algozzine, B. (2006). Research on reading instruction for individuals with significant cognitive disabilities. *Exceptional Children, 72,* 392–408.

Brulle, C. G. (1994). Elementary school student responses to teacher directions. *Education and Treatment of Children, 17,* 459–467.

Bryant, P. E., Bradley, L., & Maclean, M. (1989). Nursery rhymes, phonological skills, and reading. *Journal of Child Language, 16,* 407–428.

Burns, B. (1999). *The mindful school: How to teach balanced reading and writing.* Upper Saddle River, NJ: Merrill/Prentice Hall.

Bursuck, W., Polloway, E. A., Plante, L., Epstein, M. H., Jayanthi, M., & McConeghy, J. (1996). Report card grading and adaptations: A national survey of classroom practices. *Exceptional Children, 62,* 301–305.

Burton, A. W., & Rodgerson, R. W. (2001). New perspectives on the assessment of movement skills and motor abilities. *Adapted Physical Activity Quarterly, 18*(4), 347–365.

Campbell, P. S., & Scott-Kassner, C. (1995). *Music in childhood: From preschool through the elementary grades.* New York: Schirmer.

Case-Smith, J. (1996). Half-pint smarts. *American Journal of Occupational Therapy, 49,* 39–40.

Cavalier, A., Ferretti, R. P., Hodges, A. E., Cavalier, A., Ferretti, R. P., & Hodges, A. E. (1997). Self-management within a classroom token economy for students with learning disabilities. *Research in Developmental Disabilities, 18,* 167–178.

Chesapeake Institute. (1994). *Attention deficit disorder: What teachers should know.* Washington, DC: Division of Innovation and Development Office of Special Education Programs, Office of Special Education and Rehabilitative Services, U.S. Department of Education. (ERIC Document Reproduction Service No. ED370336)

Chesapeake Institute & Widmeyer Group. (1994). *101 ways to help children with ADD learn: Tips from successful teachers.* Washington, DC: Division of Innovation and Development, Office of Special Education Programs, Office of Special Education and Rehabilitative Services, U.S. Department of Education. (ERIC Document Reproduction Service No. ED389109)

Cornoldi, C., Rigoni, F., Thessoldi, P. E., & Vio, C. (1999). Imagery deficits in nonverbal learning disabilities. *Journal of Learning Disabilities, 32,* 48–58.

Coyne, M. D., Sipoli, R. P., & Ruby, M. F. (2006). Beginning reading instruction for students at risk for reading disabilities: What, how, and when. *Intervention in School and Clinic, 41,* 161–168.

Cunningham, P. (1998). How tutoring works. *Instructor, 107,* 36.

Daniels, H., Zemelman, S., & Bizar, M. (1999). Whole language works: Sixty years of research. *Educational Leadership, 57*(2), 32–36.

De La Paz, S., & Graham, S. (1997). Strategy instruction in planning: Effects on the writing performance and behavior of students. *Exceptional Children, 63,* 167–181.

Desrochers, J. (1999). Vision problems: How teachers can help. *Young Children, 54*(2), 36–38.

Dockrell, J. E., Lindsay, G., Connelly, V., & Mackie, C. (2007). Constraints in the production of written text in children with specific language impairments. *Exceptional Children, 73,* 147–164.

Dunton, J. (1998). The four Bs of classroom management. *Techniques: Making Education and Career Connections, 73,* 32–33.

Eastman, B. G., & Rasbury, W. C. (1981). Cognitive self-instruction for the control of impulsive classroom behavior: Ensuring the treatment package. *Journal of Abnormal Child Psychology, 93,* 381–387.

Educational Resources Information Center. (1998). *Teaching children with attention deficit/hyperactivity disorder.* Reston, VA: ERIC Clearinghouse on Disabilities and Gifted Education, Council for Exceptional Children. (ERIC Document Reproduction Service No. ED423633)

Edyburn, D. L. (2000). Assistive technology and students with mild disabilities. *Focus on Exceptional Children, 32*(9), 1–22.

Elksnin, L. (1997). Collaborative speech and language services for students with learning disabilities. *The Journal of Learning Disabilities, 30,* 414–426.

Enright, D. S., & Gomez, B. (1985). PRO-ACT: Six strategies for organizing peer interaction in elementary classrooms. *The Journal for the National Association for Bilingual Education, 9*(3), 5–24.

Epstein, M., Polloway, E., Buck, G., Bursuck, W., Wissinger, L., Whitehouse, F., et al. (1997). Homework-related communication problems: Perspectives of general education teachers. *Learning Disabilities Research and Practice, 12,* 221–227.

Erdmann, L. (1994). *Success at last.* Portsmouth, NH: Heinemann.

Forgan, J. W., & Gonzales-DeHass, A. (2004). How to infuse social skills training into literacy instruction. *Teaching Exceptional Children, 36*(6), 24–30.

Friedland, E. S., & Truesdell, K. S. (2006). "I can read to whoever wants to hear me read": Buddy readers speak out with confidence. *Teaching Exceptional Children, 38*(5), 36–42.

Fuchs, D., Fuchs, L. S., & Compton, D. L. (2004). Identifying reading disabilities by responsiveness-to-instruction: Specifying measures and criteria. *Learning Disability Quarterly, 27,* 216–228.

Fuchs, D., Fuchs, L. S., McMaster, K. L., Yen, L., & Svenson, E. (2004). Nonresponders: How to find them? How to help them? What do they mean for special education? *Teaching Exceptional Children, 37*(1), 72–77.

Fuchs, D., Fuchs, L. S., Thompson, A., Al Otaiba, S., Yen, L., Yang, N. J., et al. (2002). Exploring the importance of reading programs for kindergartners with disabilities in mainstream classrooms. *Exceptional Children, 68,* 295–311.

Fuchs, L. S., Compton, D. L., Fuchs, D., Paulsen, K., Bryant, J., & Hamlett, C. L. (2005). Responsiveness to intervention: Preventing and identifying mathematics disability. *Teaching Exceptional Children, 37*(4), 60–63.

Fuchs, L. S., Fuchs, D., & Compton, D. L. (2004). Monitoring early reading development in first grade: Word identification fluency versus nonsense word fluency. *Exceptional Children, 71,* 7–21.

Fuchs, L. S., Fuchs, D., Hamlett, C. L., Hope, S. K., Hollenbeck, K. N., Capizzi, A. M., et al. (2006). Extending responsiveness-to-intervention to math problem solving at third grade. *Teaching Exceptional Children, 38*(4), 59–63.

Fuchs, L. S., Fuchs, D., Prentice, K., Burch, M., & Paulsen, K. (2002). Hot math: Promoting mathematical problem solving among third-grade students with disabilities. *Teaching Exceptional Children, 35*(1), 70–73.

Fulk, B. M., Lohman, D., & Belfiore, P. J. (1997). Effects of integrated picture mnemonics on the letter recognition and letter-sound acquisition of transitional first-grade students with special needs. *Learning Disability Quarterly, 20,* 33–42.

Garcia, T. (2007). Facilitating the reading process. *Teaching Exceptional Children, 39*(3), 12–17.

Gately, S. E. (2004). Developing concept of word: The work of emergent readers. *Teaching Exceptional Children, 36*(6), 16–22.

Gerber, A., & Klein, E. R. (2004). A speech-language approach to early reading success. *Teaching Exceptional Children, 36*(6), 8–14.

Getch, Y., Bhukhanwala, F., & Neuharth-Pritchett, S. (2007). Strategies for helping children with diabetes in elementary and middle schools. *Teaching Exceptional Children, 39*(3), 46–51.

Gfeller, K. (1989). Behavior disorders: Strategies for the music teacher. *Music Educators Journal, 7,* 27–30.

Ghaziuddin, M., Leininger, L., & Tsai, L. (1995). Brief report: Thought disorder in Asperger syndrome; Comparison with high-functioning autism. *Journal of Autism and Developmental Disorders, 25,* 311–317.

Gibson, D., Haeberli, F. B., & Glover, T. A. (2005). Use of recommended and provided testing accommodations. *Assessment for Effective Intervention, 31,* 19–36.

Hebert, E. A. (1998). Lessons learned about student portfolios. *Phi Delta Kappan, 80,* 583–585.

Hernandez, H. (1997). *Teaching in multicultural classrooms: A teacher's guide to context, process, and content.* New York: Simon and Schuster.

Higgins, E. L., & Raskind, Marshall H. (1995). Compensatory effectiveness of speech recognition on the written composition performance of post-secondary students with learning disabilities. *Learning Disabilities Quarterly, 18,* 159–174.

Hitchcock, C. H., Prater, M. A., & Dowrick, P. W. (2004). Reading comprehension and fluency: Examining the effects of tutoring and video self-modeling on first-grade students with reading difficulties. *Learning Disability Quarterly, 27,* 89–103.

Holzberg, C. S. (1995). Beyond the printed book. *Technology and Learning, 15,* 22–23.

How to manage your students with ADD/ADHD. (1997). *Instructor, 106*(6), 63–65.

Huang, A., Mellblom, C., & Pearman, E. (1997). Inclusion of all students: Concerns and incentives of educators. *Education and Training in Mental Retardation and Developmental Disabilities, 32,* 11–20.

Huber, J. (1997). Laptop word processor: A way to close the technology gap. *Technology Connection, 4*(2), 26–28.

Hudson, P. (1997). Using teacher-guided practice to help students with learning disabilities acquire and retain social studies content. *Learning Disability Quarterly, 20,* 23–32.

Humpal, M. E., & Dimmick, J. A. (1995). Special learners in the music classroom. *Music Educators Journal, 81,* 21–23.

Hurd, D. W. (1997). Novelty and its relation to field trips. *Education, 118,* 29–35.

James, L. A., Abbot, M., & Greenwood, C. R. (2001). How Adam became a writer: Winning writing strategies for low-achieving students. *Teaching Exceptional Children, 33*(3), 30–37.

Jitendra, A. K. (2002). Teaching students math problem-resolving through graphic representations. *Teaching Exceptional Children, 34*(4), 34–38.

Jitendra, A. K., Rohena-Diaz, E., & Nolet, V. (1998). A dynamic curriculum-based language assessment. *Preventing School Failure, 42,* 182–185.

Johnson, D. (1990). Why can't my student learn like everyone else? *Adult Learning, 2*(2), 24–25, 28.

Johnson, G. M. (1999). Inclusive education: Fundamental instructional strategies and considerations. *Preventing School Failure, 43,* 72.

Johnson, K. K. (1998). Teaching Shakespeare to learning disabled students. *English Journal, 83,* 45.

Justice, L. M., & Kaderavek, J. (2002). Using shared storybook reading to promote emergent literacy. *Teaching Exceptional Children, 34*(4), 8–13.

Kameenui, E. J., & Carnine, D. W. (1998). Effective strategies that accommodate diverse learners. Columbus, OH: Merrill/Prentice Hall.

Kleinert, H. L., Kennedy, S., & Kearns, J. F. (1999). The impact of alternate assessments: A statewide teacher survey. *The Journal of Special Education, 33,* 93–102.

Korinek, L. (1993). Positive behavior management: Fostering responsible student behavior. In B. S. Billingsley (with D. Peterson, D. Bodkins, & M. B. Hendricks), *Program leadership for serving students with disabilities* (pp. 263–298). Blacksburg and Richmond: Virginia Polytechnic Institute and State University and Virginia State Department of Education. (ERIC Document Reproduction Service No. ED372537)

Kowalski, E., Lieberman, L., Pucci, G., & Mulawka, C. (2005). Implementing IEP or 504 goals and objectives into general physical education. *The Journal of Physical Education, Recreation, & Dance, 76*(7), 33–37.

Lane, K. L., Graham, S., Harris, K. R., & Weisenbach, J. L. (2006). Teaching writing strategies to young students struggling with writing and at risk for behavioral disorders: Self-regulated strategy development. *Teaching Exceptional Children, 39*(1), 60–64.

Lee, Y. J. (2006). The process-oriented ESL writing assessment: Promises and challenges. *Journal of Second Language Writing, 15,* 307–330.

Lewis, M., Wray, D., & Rospigliosi, P. (1994). Making reading for information more accessible to children with learning difficulties. *Support for Learning, 9,* 155–161.

Logan, K. R. (1998). Comparing instructional contexts of students with and without severe disabilities in general education classrooms. *Exceptional Children, 64,* 343–358.

Lombardi, T., & Butera, G. (1998). Mnemonics: Strengthening thinking skills of students with special needs. *The Clearing House, 71,* 284–287.

MacArthur, C., Graham, S., & Schwartz, S. (1995). Evaluation of a writing instruction model that integrated a process approach, strategy instruction, and word processing. *Learning Disability Quarterly, 18,* 278–294.

Majsterek, D. J. (1990). Writing disabilities: Is word processing the answer? *Intervention in School and Clinic, 26*(2), 93–97.

Malloy, W. (1997). Responsible inclusion: Celebrating diversity and academic excellence. *NASSP Bulletin, 81,* 80–85.

Manzo, A. V., Manzo, U. C., & Thomas, M. M. (2006). Rationale for systematic vocabulary development: Antidote for state mandates. *Journal of Adolescent & Adult Literacy, 49,* 610–619.

Marek-Schroer, M. F., & Schroer, N. A. (1993). Identifying and providing for musically gifted young children. *Roeper Review, 16*(1), 33–36.

Martinez-Roldan, C. M., & Lopez-Robertson, J. M. (2000). Initiating literature circles in a first grade bilingual classroom. *The Reading Teacher, 53,* 270–281.

Mastropieri, M. A., & Scruggs, T. E. (1997). Best practices in promoting reading comprehension in students with learning disabilities. *Remedial and Special Education, 18,* 197–213.

McEwan, E. K. (1998). *The ADHD intervention checklist.* Thousand Oaks, CA: Corwin Press.

McKinney, J. D., Montague, M., & Hocutt, A. M. (1993). Educational assessment of students with ADD. *Exceptional Children, 60,* 125–133.

McLoughlin, J. A., & Lewis, R. B. (1994). *Assessing special students.* New York: Macmillan.

McNaughton, D. (1994). Spelling instruction for students with learning disabilities: Implications for research and practice. *Learning Disability Quarterly, 17,* 169–185.

McReynolds, J. C. (1988). Helping visually impaired students succeed in band. *Music Educators Journal, 71,* 35–38.

Meisels, S. J. (1997). Using work sampling in authentic assessments. *Educational Leadership, 54*(4), 60–65.

Michaels, C. A., Brown, F., & Mirabella, N. (2005). Personal paradigm shifts in PBS experts: Perceptions of treatment acceptability of decelerative consequence-based behavioral procedures. *Journal of Positive Behavioral Supports, 7,* 93–108.

Miller, S. P., & Hudson, P. J. (2006). Helping students with disabilities understand what mathematics means. *Teaching Exceptional Children, 39*(1), 28–35.

Montello, L., & Coons, E. E. (1998). Effects of active versus passive group music therapy on preadolescents with emotional, learning, and behavioral disorders. *Journal of Music Therapy, 35*(1), 49–67.

Monty, N. D. (1997). Transforming student assessment. *Phi Delta Kappan, 79,* 30–40, 58.

Moore, A. (1996). Assessing young readers: Questions of culture and ability. *Language Arts, 73,* 306–316.

Morgan, M., & Moni, K. B. (2005). Use phonics activities to motivate learners with difficulties. *Intervention in School and Clinic, 41*(1), 42–45.

Morgan, P. L., & Fuchs, D. (2007). Is there a bidirectional relationship between children's reading skills and reading motivation? *Exceptional Children, 73,* 165–183.

Moxley, R. A. (1998). Treatment-only designs and student self-recording as strategies for public school teachers. *Education and Treatment of Children, 21*(1), 37–61.

National Board for Professional Teaching Standards. (2008). *The standards.* Retrieved January 6, 2008, from http://www.nbpts.org/the_standards

National Joint Committee on Learning Disabilities. (1993). Providing appropriate education for students with learning disabilities in regular education classrooms. *Journal of Learning Disabilities, 26,* 330–332.

Newman, J. (1998). *Tensions of teaching: Beyond tips to critical reflection.* New York: Teachers College Press.

Novelli, J. (1997). Seating solutions. *Primary Instructor, 107*(2), 78–79.

Olinghouse, N. G., Lambert, W., & Compton, D. L. (2006). Monitoring children with reading disabilities' response to phonics intervention: Are there differences between intervention aligned and general skill progress monitoring assessments? *Exceptional Children, 73,* 90–106.

Ormond, J. E. (1998). *Educational psychology: Developing learners* (2nd ed.). Upper Saddle River, NJ: Prentice Hall.

Ortiz, A. A. (1997). Learning disabilities occurring concomitantly with linguistic differences. *Journal of Learning Disabilities, 30,* 321–332.

Patzer, C. E., & Pettegrew, B. S. (1996). Finding a voice: Primary students with developmental disabilities express personal meanings through writing. *Teaching Exceptional Children, 29*(2), 22–27.

Perry, L. A. (1997). Using wordless picture books with beginning readers (of any age). *Teaching Exceptional Children, 29*(3), 68–69.

Pfiffner, L. J. (1998). *All about ADHD: The complete practical guide for classroom teachers.* New York: Scholastic Books.

Quinn, M. M., Gable, R. A., Rutherford, R. B., Nelson, C. M., & Howell, K. W. (1998). *Addressing student problem behavior: An IEP team's introduction to functional behavior assessment and behavior intervention plans* (2nd ed.). Washington, DC: American Institute for Research: Center for Effective Collaboration and Practice.

Raver, S. A. (2004). Monitoring child progress in early childhood special education settings. *Teaching Exceptional Children, 36*(6), 52–57.

Reason, R. (1999). ADHD: A psychological response to an evolving concept. *Journal of Learning Disabilities, 32,* 85–91.

Reis, S. M., Burns, D. E., & Renzulli, J. S. (1995). *Curriculum compacting: The complete guide to modifying the regular curriculum for high ability students.* Mansfield Center, CT: Creative Learning Press.

Riccomini, P. J. (2005). Identification and remediation of systematic error patterns in subtraction. *Learning Disability Quarterly, 28,* 233–242.

Richardson, C. (1990). Measuring musical giftedness. *Music Education Journal, 76,* 40.

Riley, G., Beard, L. A., & Strain, J. (2004). Assistive technology at use in the teacher education programs at Jacksonville State University. *TechTrends: Linking Research & Practice to Improve Learning, 48*(6), 47–49.

Ritchey, K. D. (2006). Learning to write: Progress-monitoring tolls for beginning and at-risk writers. *Teaching Exceptional Children, 39*(2), 22–26.

Robinson, M. (1995). Alternative assessment techniques for teachers. *Music Educators Journal, 81,* 28–34.

Rock, E. E., Fessler, M. A., & Church, R. P. (1997). The concomitance of learning disabilities and emotional/behavioral disorders: A conceptual model. *Journal of Learning Disabilities, 30,* 245–260.

Rodriguez, D., Parmar, R. S., & Signer, B. R. (2001). Fourth-grade culturally and linguistically diverse exceptional students' concepts of number line. *Exceptional Children, 67,* 199–210.

Rosner, J. (1993). *Helping children overcome learning difficulties* (3rd ed.). New York: Walker.

Ryba, K., Selby, L., & Nolan, P. (1995). Computers empower students with special needs. *Educational Leadership, 53,* 82–84.

Saddler, B., & Preschern, J. (2007). Improving sentence-writing ability through sentence-combining practice. *Teaching Exceptional Children, 39*(3), 6–11.

Saenz, L. M., Fuchs, L. S., & Fuchs, D. (2005). Peer-assisted learning strategies for English language learners with learning disabilities. *Exceptional Children, 71,* 231–247.

Salend, S., & Salend, S. J. (1985). Adapting teacher-made tests for mainstreamed students. *Journal of Learning Disabilities, 18,* 373–375.

Schoen, S. F., & Bullard, M. (2002). Action research during recess: A time for children with autism to play and learn. *Teaching Exceptional Children, 35*(1), 36–39.

Schubert, A. (1997). I want to talk like everyone. *Mental Retardation, 35,* 347–354.

Siege, L. S. (1995). Issues in the definition and diagnosis of learning disabilities: A perspective on *Guckenberger v. Boston University. Journal of Learning Disabilities, 32*(4), 304–319.

Siegel-Causey, E., & Allinder, R. M. (1998). Using alternative assessment for students with severe disabilities: Alignment with best practices. *Educational Training in Mental Retardation and Developmental Disabilities, 33*(2), 168–178.

Simmons, D. C., Fuchs, L. S., Fuchs, D., & Mathes, P. (1995). Effects of explicit teaching and peer tutoring on the reading achievement of learning disabled and low-performing students in regular classrooms. *Elementary School Journal, 95,* 387–408.

Simmons, D. C., Fuchs, L. S., Fuchs, D., Mathes, P., & Hodge, P. (1994). How inclusion built a community of learners. *Educational Leadership, 52,* 42–43.

Skau, L., & Cascella, P. W. (2006). Using assistive technology to foster speech and language skills at home and in preschool. *Teaching Exceptional Children, 38*(6), 12–17.

Slavin, R. E. (1996). Neverstreaming: Preventing learning disabilities. *Educational Leadership, 53*(5), 4–7.

Smaligo, M. A. (1998). Resources for helping blind music students. *Music Educators Journal, 85,* 23–26.

Smith, S. B., Baker, S., & Oudeans, M. K. (2001). Making a difference in the classroom with early literacy instruction. *Teaching Exceptional Children, 33*(6), 8–14.

Sutman, F., et al. (1993). *Teaching science effectively to limited English proficient students* (ERIC/CUE Digest, #87). New York: ERIC Clearinghouse on Urban Education. (ERIC Document Reproduction Service No. ED357113)

Taylor, H. E., & Larson, S. (1998). Teaching children with ADHD: What do elementary and middle school social studies teachers need to know. *Social Studies, 89,* 161–164.

Therrien, W. J., & Kubina, R. M. (2006). Developing reading fluency with repeated reading. *Intervention in School and Clinic, 41,* 156–160.

Thompson, A. (1996). Attention deficit hyperactivity disorder: A parent's perspective. *Phi Delta Kappan, 6,* 433–436.

Thompson, S. (1996). *Nonverbal learning disorders.* Retrieved June 26, 2007, from http://www.ldonline.org/article/6114

Thurlow, M. L., Ysseldyke, J. E., & Silverstein, B. (1995). Testing accommodations for students with disabilities. *Remedial and Special Education, 16,* 260–270.

Tindal, G., & Parker, R. (1989). Assessment of written expression for students in compensatory and special education programs. *The Journal of Special Education, 23,* 169–183.

Torgesen, H. K., & Murphey, H. A. (1979). Verbal vs. nonverbal and complex vs. simple responses in the paired-associate learning of poor readers. *Journal of General Psychology, 101,* 219–226.

Tripp, A., Rizzo, T. L., & Webbert, L. (2007). Inclusion in physical education: Changing the culture. *The Journal of Physical Education, Recreation, & Dance, 78*(2), 32–48.

Turnbull, A. P., Rutherford, H., Turnbull, R., Shank, M., & Leal, D. (1995). *Exceptional lives: Special education in today's schools.* Upper Saddle River, NJ: Prentice Hall.

Uhry, J. K., & Shepard, M. J. (1997). Teaching phonological recoding to young children with phonological processing deficits: The effect on sight-vocabulary acquisition. *Learning Disability Quarterly, 20,* 104–125.

Vallecorsa, A. L., & deBettencourt, L. (1997). Using a mapping procedure to teach reading and writing skills to middle grade students with learning disabilities. *Education and Treatment of Children, 20,* 173–188.

Vaughn, S., Elbaum, B., Schumm, J., & Hughes, M. (1998). Social outcomes for students with and without learning disabilities. *Journal of Learning Disabilities, 31,* 428–436.

Vaughn, S., Linan-Thompson, S., Kouzekanani, K., Bryant, D. P., Dickson, S., & Blozis, S. A. (2003). Reading instruction grouping for students with reading difficulties. *Remedial and Special Education, 24,* 301–315.

Voltz, D., Dooley, E., & Jeffries, P. (1999). Preparing special educators for cultural diversity: How far have we come. *Teacher Education and Special Education, 22,* 66–77.

Wadlington, E., Jacob, S., & Bailey, S. (1996). Teaching students with dyslexia in the regular classroom. *Childhood Education, 73,* 5.

Walczyk, E. B. (1993). Music instruction and the hearing impaired. *Music Educators Journal, 80,* 42–44.

Walker, L. M. (1993). Academic learning in an integrated setting for hearing-impaired students: A description of an Australian unit's efforts to meet the challenge. *The Volta Review, 95,* 295–304.

Welsch, R. G. (2006). 20 ways to increase oral reading fluency. *Intervention in School and Clinic, 41,* 180–183.

Whitaker, S. D., Harvey, M., Hassell, L. J., Linder, T., & Tutterrow, D. (2006). The fish strategy: Moving from sight words to decoding. *Teaching Exceptional Children, 38*(5), 14–18.

Williams, J. P. (2005). At-risk second graders can improve their comprehension of compare/contrast text. *Teaching Exceptional Children, 37*(3), 58–61.

Williams, J. P., Hall, K. M., Lauer, K. D., & Lord, K. M. (2001). Helping elementary school children understand story themes. *Teaching Exceptional Children, 33*(6), 75–77.

Wilson, G. L. (2004). Using videotherapy to access curriculum and enhance growth. *Teaching Exceptional Children, 36*(6), 32–37.

Wilson, R. (1996). Teachers building self-esteem in students. *The Delta Kappa Gamma Bulletin, 62,* 43–48.

Wolery, M., Katzenmeyer, A. L., Snyder, E. D., & Werts, M. D. (1997). Training elementary teachers to embed instruction during classroom activities. *Education and Treatment of Children, 20*(1), 40–58.

Xin, Y. P., & Jittendra, A. K. (1999). The effects of instruction in solving mathematical word problems for students with special learning problems: A meta-analysis. *The Journal of Special Education, 32,* 207–225.

Yoo, S-Y. (1997). Children's literature for developing good readers and writers in kindergarten. *Education/ Print Source Plus, 118,* 123–128.

Ysseldyke, J. E., & Algozzine, B. (1995). *Special education: A practical approach for teachers* (3rd ed.). Boston: Houghton Mifflin.

Zentall, S. S., Smith, Y. N., Lee, Y. B., & Wieczorek, C. (1994). Mathematical outcomes of attention-deficit hyperactivity disorder. *Journal of Learning Disabilities, 27,* 510–519.

Zhang, J. (2003). Effective instructional procedures for teaching individuals with severe disabilities in motor skills. *Perceptual & Motor Skills, 97*(2), 547–559.

Index

CORWIN PRESS

The Corwin Press logo—a raven striding across an open book—represents the union of courage and learning. Corwin Press is committed to improving education for all learners by publishing books and other professional development resources for those serving the field of PreK–12 education. By providing practical, hands-on materials, Corwin Press continues to carry out the promise of its motto: **"Helping Educators Do Their Work Better."**